SAYING
GOODBYE TO
DISAPPOINTMENTS

SAYING GOODBYE TO DISAPPOINTMENTS

*Finding Hope
When Our Dreams
Don't Come True*

Jan Stoop
and
Dr. David Stoop

A
JANET
THOMA
BOOK

THOMAS NELSON PUBLISHERS
Nashville

Published in association with the literary agency of Alive Communications, P.O. Box 49068, Colorado Springs, CO 80949.

Published in Nashville, Tennessee, by Janet Thoma Books, a division of Thomas Nelson, Inc., Publishers, and distributed in Canada by Word Communications, Ltd., Richmond, British Columbia, and in the United Kingdom by Word (UK), Ltd., Milton Keynes, England.

Library of Congress Cataloging-in-Publication Data

Stoop, David A.
  Saying goodbye to disappointments / David Stoop and Jan Stoop.
    p. cm.
  "A Janet Thoma book."
  ISBN 0-8407-6741-2
  1. Disappointment. 2. Disappointment—Case studies.
3. Adjustment (Psychology) I. Title.
BF575.D57S86 1993
155.2'4—dc20   93-19118
                                                    CIP

Printed in the United States of America

1 2 3 4 5 6 — 98 97 96 95 94 93

Acknowledgements

Our sincere thanks to Janet Thoma, Kay Strom, Martha Kimmel Greene, and Susan Salmon Trotman, for their expertise and help in bringing this book together.

And to all the women who completed our surveys and talked with us about their disappointments—our gratitude for bringing these ideas to life!

Contents

"Disappointment is the lot of women. It shall be the business of my life to deepen this disappointment in every woman's heart until she bows down to it no longer."
Lucy Stone, 1855

— PART I —

From Dream to Disappointment

— 1 —

Great Expectations

T he promised box arrived much earlier than planned. The neighbors had left it on Jan's family's front porch, being careful not to embarrass them by letting other neighbors know they were accepting help. Jan waited impatiently while her mom called down to her dad's car repair shop, which was located just underneath the front half of their modest home.

"Can someone come up here? We need help with the box," she yelled. Jan's older brother quickly ran up the steps and took the box inside the house.

The box was larger than usual. Six-year-old Jan couldn't contain the excitement she felt. As the youngest of five children, she was familiar with the box routine, but she was just as excited to open this new box of used clothing as she had been to open the very first one. Her brother was disgusted at her display of enthusiasm. "Settle down!" he warned. "Why do you always have to dance around like that?"

Jan ignored his admonition. "Hurry, hurry," she pleaded. "Get the knife and cut the string." When he didn't move quickly, she added, "I'll get the knife!"

"No, you won't! I'll get it!" he said as he headed for the front door. The neighbors who had delivered the box had already gone through the contents. They always took the best items, but since it was their wealthy relatives who had given the used clothes away, they had a right to choose first. Besides, Jan's family didn't mind too much; they were delighted to have an opportunity to choose from the leftovers.

Jan's family was not unlike many other families who had to struggle for the bare necessities in the 1940s. Jan remembers her mom sewing shirts for her dad and two brothers from the corduroy used to upholster car seats. Once washed and pressed, these shirts were given as special gifts for birthdays and holidays since clothing was not easy to come by.

Jan could hardly contain her excitement and anticipation about what was in the box. "Open it, hurry, please!" she pleaded when her brother returned with the knife.

"The more you ask me to hurry, the longer it will take me," her brother said as he proceeded to cut one string at a time. This back-and-forth chatter was part of their special brother-sister routine. The more Jan asked him, the slower he moved.

After what seemed like an eternity to Jan, her brother let her open the flaps of the well-worn box. Jan's mom had already lost interest in their arguing and had gone back to check on something in the kitchen. Her big sisters were away at college, so Jan didn't have to worry about them getting first pick.

Jan peeked inside the box. Right on top was a pink taffeta dress with silk flowers pinned to the waist! As she started to reach for it, her brother goaded, "Too big for you, little girl!" and he snatched it away.

Fuzzy angora sweaters were next. "Not for you," Jan's brother smugly said.

Then he pulled out a few well-worn blouses, three thick blankets, a frilly apron, and two print housedresses. "Mom, here's something for you," he called. Finally, he closed the flaps on the box and said, "That's it! All there is! Nothing for you this time!"

"Just let me see, please—pretty please! I want to see if it is really empty," Jan begged, even though she knew better. In their brother-sister game this was always his signal to withhold whatever she wanted and tease her further. Finally, she yelled, "Mom, he won't let me see!"

Jan's mom intervened and made Jan's brother let her look into the box. The dark ball in the bottom didn't look like much, but Jan reached in and took it out carefully. She held it up so she could look at it.

The most beautiful snowsuit I've ever seen, Jan thought with delight. *Truly worth the fight!* It had zippered leggings and a princess-style coat with a flared bottom. The fabric was the deepest color of burgundy velvet she had ever seen. But that was not all. Soft white fur trimmed the hemline of the coat and the cuffs. Even the buttons were made of fur, and a matching hat was trimmed with the same fur and velvet ties.

I can't believe it! Jan thought. The velvet snowsuit looked a little large for her, but that wouldn't be a problem. At worst she could grow into it. *The snowsuit's mine!* She turned to her brother and sang, "It's mine, it's mine!"

Of course, he said he thought it was the ugliest thing he had ever seen, and he didn't think any girl in her right mind would be caught dead in it. But Jan didn't care what he said. It was beautiful, and it was hers!

Mom was almost as excited as Jan was. She wondered why their neighbors had not taken the snowsuit for themselves. "Maybe they didn't see it there in the bottom of the box?"

Yes, that's it, Jan told herself as she raced off to her room to put it on. *And they missed it because it was for me, just for me.*

The spring afternoon was warm, but Jan didn't care. She put on the burgundy velvet snowsuit and scooted down the steps to show her dad. He was busy at work, but he laid down the automobile part he was working on and took a good look at her.

"Do you like it, Dad? Do you like it?"

"You look splendid!" he replied with a smile.

Her mom had followed her to the garage, and she joined Dad in his praise. Then she added, "Now get back upstairs and take that off before you get it dirty. And hang it up somewhere!"

Hang it up? Jan wondered. *Where can I hang this precious outfit so it will never get dirty or crushed?* Finally she settled on the hook on the back of the door to her room.

Every night after that, as Jan lay in bed, she could see the snowsuit and think about when and where she might wear it. *Will there ever be an occasion special enough?* she wondered. It was too beautiful to wear to school or to play in the snow. Maybe someday, at the right time and in the right place, she would wear it. She would wait until then. In the meantime, she would dream about her beautiful snowsuit. In her dreams she would be an elegant princess, draped in velvet and fur. Or maybe she would live in a mansion with a winding staircase and massive rooms. Maybe the outfit meant she would be famous and influential and have a special place in history!

I will save this snowsuit forever, she determined.

One day, several weeks later, Jan was swinging on the glider on the back porch of their house, playing with her dolls and sorting out scraps of fabric her mom would use to make some new doll clothes. Suddenly, a loud explosion shook every part of their two-story, brick house. Thick, dark, billowy smoke—the kind that could only come from some terrible occurrence—came from her dad's repair shop under the house.

Jan ran to open the screen door to the kitchen. *Surely there is something I can do,* she thought.

But people were yelling at her from all directions. "Don't go in there!"

She felt confused. What should she do? Many precious things—her kitten, her toys, her special doll house—were in there. And Mom and Dad—where were they? Then she thought of the burgundy velvet snowsuit.

I'll have to go in, just for a second, she decided. Jan looked around to see who was yelling at her, and then reached for the screen door again.

But it was too late! Red flames came rushing through the door. *My beautiful snowsuit! Surely it will be okay. It wouldn't be burned!* she reassured herself as she stepped back.

Her mom and dad and brother got out of the burning house without a scratch. Even her kitten miraculously clawed its way through the screen on the kitchen door. Nothing else survived the fire, however. Nothing could be salvaged. Fueled by the gasoline and paint stored in the shop, the fire was so hot that the coins from Jan's piggy bank melted into a solid mass.

Days later, as the family sorrowfully sifted through the cooling remains, they still hoped they would find something. Jan's mom and dad combed the ruins for any sign of a family photograph—even a small corner of one. But there was none.

Maybe I can find something from my room—a toy, a game piece, any souvenir to remind me: this was my place. But there was nothing.

Most of all, Jan hoped for a small trace of the burgundy velvet snowsuit. She searched frantically. She had imagined it would be safe, hanging on the back of her bedroom door. After all, she reasoned, things are supposed to be safe when you take care of them. Mom said so. But the velvet snowsuit was not safe and now it was gone. Forever.

That was one of Jan's first disappointments, and it was not the last. Like all women (and men, for that matter), she has experienced many disappointments, many times when her dreams didn't come true.

DISAPPOINTED WOMEN

Jan recalls that, when she was a child, there were days when her mother would go quietly to her room. Later, when her mother came out, Jan knew she had been crying because of the puffiness around her eyes. Jan often wondered, *What has she been crying about? What's wrong?* It was all so mysterious. No one ever talked about what bothered her mom; Jan's childlike deduction was: *Maybe I did something to cause the sadness.*

Jan seldom asked if that were the case, but when she did, her mom protested. "No, it's not you. It's a lot of things. . . . Someday you will understand."

Now Jan thinks she is beginning to understand. As she lives out her adult years, she agrees, "It's a lot of things—my marriage, my family, myself."

That same malaise was expressed years ago by Lucy Stone, a leader in the women's suffrage movement, who said in a speech in 1855, "In education, in marriage, in religion, in everything, disappointment is the lot of women. It shall be the business of my life to deepen this disappointment in every woman's heart until she bows down to it no longer."[1]

Is disappointment the lot of women? We think so; at least it seems to be for the women who come into our counseling offices and those we surveyed.

We have a little room in the upstairs of our home where both of us like to sit and write or do paperwork. One balmy day Jan opened the doors that led from that room out to the tiny balcony. She sat down, propped her feet up on the edge of the couch, and contemplated her life.

What's wrong with me? What's wrong with the women we counsel? she wondered as she looked out the window at the row of nice, yet similar and boring, houses that lined the street of our neighborhood. *I have it pretty good. A lot of women would gladly trade places with me,* she told herself. But she knew something was going on deep down inside of her—and other women—that she couldn't ignore any longer: a familiar, haunting sense of unrest and dissatisfaction with life. *Things are not as I planned, not as I wished them to be,* she admitted. *But if I recognize that unrest, or give words to it, will I be sorry? Will this tempest of disappointments overtake me if I look carefully at it?*

As she wrestled with questions like these in our upstairs room, Jan wanted to shout out to herself, *Okay, okay. I'm paying attention. But what am I supposed to pay attention to?* That day Jan began to count her losses. Yes, she knew it was far more acceptable to count her blessings, but the losses were there, and she could no longer ignore them. The loss of the snowsuit was just the beginning. In her mind she listed the events that had disappointed her, caused her deep pain, and greatly affected the direction of her life. There had been many losses, she discovered.

Some of them were a result of the disturbing choices others in her life had made, some came from painfully unexpected circumstances, and others, she had to admit, came from her own choices and failures. But as she had done so many times before, she asked herself, *Why can't I just get my act together, accept the losses, and get on with life?*

That day Jan decided, *Something has to change. I can't go on dealing with disappointment in the same old way.* She began to realize that each disappointing experience had taken its toll on her and that she was reaping the consequences emotionally and physically.

At first Jan kept this decision to herself, reviewing the losses and their effects in her mind. She was surprised at how reluctant she was to share them with anyone else. "I realized, not only did I feel guilty for having the high expectations that preceded the disappointment, but that some disappointments were so deep that I felt to reveal them was to expose the deepest secrets of who I am. They are like the covering for my feelings of anger which I cannot allow. No one will really understand the depth of my hurt."

The women we talked to in preparation for this book had many of the same feelings. They said that sometimes in the safety of a counseling office or in the presence of a trusted friend, they could verbalize a few of their disappointments. "We share a little," they said, "but we seldom let others, no matter how much they love us or how trustworthy they are, come further inside of us than the vestibule. Our inner sanctum of hurts and disappointments is protected against the judgment of others, and even against the scrutiny of our 'recovering' self. Disappointments are kept in our private place where they can be nursed and savored by no one, except occasionally by our hurting selves."

Talk it out, place it on the table, bring it out of the darkness, we are told. That will allow God's healing power to touch even the deepest disappointments. But for some of us it just isn't that simple. We grasp a few handfuls and try to bring them to the surface, and then we retreat. Jan knew the principles—"To bring things out into the light is best" and "To face the unacknowledged in us is to give voice to the damaged parts of us." But she wasn't able to apply these principles easily.

Yet, finally, Jan began to share her disappointments with Dave. When she did, she could see patterns emerge. Together they began to talk to women in their counseling offices. They distributed questionnaires to assess the extent of women's disappointment in the seminar packets of four different Minirth-Meier seminars in California and Washington in 1992. Over three hundred women took the time to complete the questionnaire. They all seemed to feel somewhat similar. "Yes, disappointment is a problem," they all agreed, as they readily filled in the blanks with information about their disappointments and what they were doing to cope with them, often adding several pages of details.

Together Jan and Dave analyzed the results of these surveys. Dave became her journeymate, her friend, her counselor as she said good-bye to her disappointments. He also began to recognize his own disappointments.

DISAPPOINTMENT DEFINED

What is disappointment? Webster defines the verb *disappoint* as "to fail to fulfill the expectations or wishes of." In Philip Yancey's book *Disappointment with God*, he defines disappointment simply as what "occurs when the actual experience of something falls far short of what we anticipate."[2]

Synonyms for the word *disappointed* include, *frustrated, baffled, circumvented, foiled,* and *ruined.* If we combine several terms to create our own definition, we could say: *Disappointment is having our dreams frustrated, circumvented, foiled, or ruined.* We could also say we have been buffaloed or baffled by someone or something we thought would help achieve our dream.

It doesn't matter if our dream is unrealistic—the wishes and hopes impossible or the expectations too high. Deep down we all say, "Someday my dream will come true." However, our dreams don't always become a reality. When they fail to materialize, we experience disappointment.

TIED TO OUR EXPECTATIONS

Dreams lead to expectations. Women with high expectations appear to be particularly susceptible to disappointments, as Colette Dowling said in her best-selling book *The Cinderella Complex*. She described the Cinderella complex as a network of largely repressed attitudes and fears that keeps women in a kind of half-light, retreating from the full use of their minds and creativity. Like Cinderella, women today are still waiting for something external to transform their lives.[3]

Women do appear to be in a waiting mode. "Sometimes we stand here in life frustrated, not knowing which way to turn, while we expect and wait for a grandma or a prince to come and fix it all," Jan says. "In the meantime our creativity is squelched as we live our lives in a dissatisfied state, searching and waiting for the fulfillment that eludes us.

"I always want to ask, 'Why?' Why is it that I expect so much in some areas, like my marriage and my home? Is it a flaw in me and in women like me who struggle with high expectations and the consequential disappointments?"

What if we could eliminate all our expectations, hopes, and dreams—would that eliminate our disappointment? Shakespeare thought so. He said, "Let not hope prevail, lest disappointment follow."

We disagree. Jan says, "I sure have tried to avoid disappointment that way. And I have talked with many women who tried, but how many of us could actually do it? It's too great a price to pay. To live without hope would eliminate any thought that our deepest desires might be met. Most of us aren't willing to live without at least a few dreams.

The women we talked to often seemed to be held hostage by the disappointments they experienced in life, even though they knew their expectations were too high. They had tried in every which way to squelch those expectations. Many of the women had vowed, as Jan did: "If my expectations make me so miserable, I will never expect again. It gets me nowhere." In effect they were saying, "I will trust no one. It only hurts when I get disappointed again." In reality they still had expectations.

We questioned why so many women tried to give up their expectations, but instead held on so tightly to their unfulfilled wishes, keeping them hidden, defended, and protected—all things that keep a destructive cycle of disappointment going, a cycle that eventually obliterates and sabotages what women really want out of life.

One woman explained it this way: "I have been so deeply disappointed so many times, I told myself early on that it didn't pay to expect anything. The painful disappointment I felt every time I expected anything good to happen was devastating. It just wasn't worth it. So I made an agreement with God—I don't expect anything anymore, and therefore I'm never disappointed. The funny thing is, down deep I know I still hope that things will be different." Her dreams are not dead. Even though deeply buried, her dreams are very much alive and exerting their influence in a surprisingly powerful way.

HOW ABOUT YOU?

You may have felt a kinship to Jan as she began to think about her disappointments. Are you struggling with disappointment? Check the statements below that apply to you.

_____ 1. I often feel lonely when others let me down.

_____ 2. I realize that many of my childhood dreams have not come true.

_____ 3. I have some hurts in my past that I keep reviewing over and over in my mind.

_____ 4. I often deny my own needs in deference to someone else's needs.

_____ 5. I have difficulty articulating any new dreams about the future.

_____ 6. Important people in my life—my husband, my kids, my friends and/or my parents—seldom meet my expectations.

_____ 7. My dreams were set aside in order to meet my husband's dreams.

_____ 8. At times no one seems to understand my sadness over my disappointments.

_____ 9. When my husband or children disappoint me, I have a hard time getting over it.

_____ 10. I regret some choices I have made.

If you checked three of these statements or fewer, you are somewhat disappointed, but you have been able to handle those disappointments fairly well. If you checked four or five, your present behavior is affected by the disappointments in your life much more than you may realize. These disappointments may be affecting the choices you confront every day, causing you to make some unwise decisions and do some unexplainable things. If you checked six or more statements, you are being overwhelmed by a pattern of disappointments and need to break the pattern.

As you read through this chapter you probably thought, *Me, too. I feel that way. So what do I do about it?*

That's what Jan asked, and that's why we wrote this book. In the last couple of years, we have been helping our patients say good-bye to their disappointments. We begin by asking them to remember their childhood dreams. Where did these dreams come from? Were they distorted to impossible proportions by factors in their childhood? We'll help you answer those questions for yourself and identify the factors that might have distorted your dreams in Part I—"From Dream to Disappointment." We will show you the links in the cycle of disappointment and how this chain can increase until it weighs us down so low we slip into depression.

In Part II—"From Disappointment to Depression"—we will help you deal with any depression you might have felt over the years when your disappointments hurt deeply and painfully. Often this depression is fueled by your unrealistic expectations, but the good news is you don't need to abandon your dreams; just readjust them. We'll show you how to do that in Part III—"From Depression to a New Hope: The Joy of Fulfillment."

We have added Personal Reflection sections at the end of some chapters. These are the exercises we give our clients to help them find hope when their dreams don't come true. These are also the exercises Jan worked through in her own journey. We suggest that you take time to apply the material in the chapter to your own life in this way.

We will begin our journey by looking at the eight major disappointments mentioned by the women who took our survey. You may think, *That's just how I feel.* Jan did as she read through the questionnaires. But do not be discouraged by those feelings. They will help you identify your own disappointments and start you down the path of dealing with them.

You can say good-bye to your disappointments. You *can* find hope and fulfillment when your dreams don't come true. Why not begin now?

—2—

What Do Women Want, Anyway?

Men often ask the question, "What do women really want?" Dave asked that question of himself, many times—and even asked Jan. She was not sure if he really wanted to know what she expected from him and from life or if he was hoping to satisfy her just by showing his concern. And Dave admits, "She's right. I felt just asking the question would do the trick. After all, we men sometimes don't do much to change the situation after that."

Books, magazines, and television shows frequently have tried to answer the question, "What do women want, anyway?" Some try to answer it by asking instead, "What do women need?" Others ask, "What do women expect?" Judith Viorst, a well-known author and columnist, focused on the question, "What do women regret?" in an article for *Redbook* magazine entitled "The Thing I Regret Most Is _____." In the article, she asked, "What are the regrets—the major regrets, the lasting regrets—that dwell in you?" The answers women gave were similar to those we got in our survey.[1]

The women in our survey were also eager to write about their disappointments. In this chapter we want to focus on the top three disappointments they listed: disappointment with their husbands and marriages, disappointments with their relationship with their dads and moms or with both parents, and disappointment with themselves.

DISAPPOINTMENT #1: HUSBANDS AND MARRIAGES

The number one disappointment, mentioned by almost half of the women we surveyed, involved their husbands and their marriages. Many women said they were married to a man who was emotionally unavailable to them. One woman put it bluntly: "He's dead on the inside." She went on to describe a husband who was preoccupied with work, sometimes hostile to her and their children, and unwilling to talk about—or even consider the importance of—the emotional issues in their relationship.

Other women said that the man they married had turned out to be someone they could not respect. One woman responded, "I feel so disappointed because my husband will not take charge of anything, not even himself. He does all right in his business, which is a bit hard for me to understand, but at home he is a total wimp. He does not stand up for anything or anyone."

When women feel disappointed in their husbands, they feel guilty. Those women who listed their husbands as being their biggest disappointment often qualified their statements with words that softened the assertion. Some said, "But, of course, I know that I have bad traits, too" or "I know that I can't really expect him to be what I need him to be" or "I feel disappointed in him, but I know it's me who needs to change."

Women described husbands who were emotionally unavailable or controlling or unfaithful. They also told of the added disappointment when more than one marriage didn't work out. Let's listen to what they said.

Emotionally Unavailable Husbands

Barbara described her situation in our survey. "Before I was married I loved my husband incredibly and trusted him completely. We had children right away—two within the first two years. Shortly after the birth of our second child, my husband told me he was a homosexual.

"At first, I was numb. I couldn't even comprehend what he was telling me. But he seemed to want help, and that was encouraging." Barbara went on to tell us about the support group they started attending and about her husband's therapy. Each step he took in the next months indicated that he might change and kept her dream to have a good marriage alive.

When her husband had been in treatment for more than two years, without anything really changing in their relationship, he told her he was HIV-positive. The alarm went off, and she couldn't silence it. He's still involved. He really hasn't changed, she thought.

Barbara struggles with her secret. She is too humiliated to tell anyone, especially her family. "So I carry the secret and all the pain that goes with it," she added. "What's so very good about life?" she asked at the end of her survey, not really expecting an answer. Her decision to seek therapy was an indication she wants to avoid the trap set by her incredible disappointment. She knows there is a lot to deal with along the road to recovery, both for her and her children, but she's on the way.

Eileen held on to her dreams, in spite of the pain. She expressed a lot of disappointment in her relationship with her father, but said, "My deepest hurt and disappointment was when my husband and I walked into the hotel on our wedding night and he said, 'If this doesn't work out, we can always get a divorce!'

"I was totally shocked. I couldn't even respond. I don't remember what happened the rest of that night—I was too dazed." Eileen went on to describe how she spent the next forty-five years trying to prove to her husband that "I'm a worthwhile person."

"Over the years, no matter what I did, it was never enough, and after forty-five years of marriage, he left me."

It has been five long, hard years since her divorce, and Eileen said, "I am just beginning to feel worthwhile as a person. I have looked deep within myself during this time. I'm beginning to see the connection between my determination to make our marriage work and the unresolved hurts with my father. I now see that over the years I was fighting against something neither my husband nor I understood."

Eileen's experience points out a factor that keeps the pain of disappointments alive, a response that began that very first night. Her husband said hurtful things ("If this doesn't work out, we can always get a divorce"), and she swallowed her feelings and tried harder and harder and harder to please him. And his hurtful comments became more hurtful each time she responded so passively.

In desperation Eileen went to see a counselor ten years before the marriage ended. "Finally I learned how to tell my husband what I needed from him. One of my counselors spent a lot of time teaching me how to use 'I' statements and how to say things assertively." She described a number of techniques she had mastered, and she had learned them all well. "But one thing I didn't learn until after the divorce is this: No matter how you tell someone what you want from them in the relationship, they aren't going to do it unless it fits their agenda.

"I never did know what my husband's agenda was, let alone how I could change it. I don't even think he knew why he was so calloused and distant."

Some women were disappointed because their husbands were so distant; others were disappointed because their husbands were so controlling.

Controlling Husbands

Men are quite creative when it comes to maintaining the control of their marriages and their wives, but their creativity depends upon their wives' cooperation. Sherrie and her husband of twenty-four years had such a relationship. She wrote, "I am an enabler and a codependent. Over the years, I have denied my husband's weaknesses, shortcomings, and lies. He keeps saying, 'It will get better,' and I keep believing him. But it never does."

As she talked about their relationship, she realized she was more disappointed in herself than in her husband. "I went back to school in order to get a better job so we could keep food on the table, and I pretended that I wanted to do these things, even enjoyed doing them. I never really let my husband know how I felt.

"One time," she added, "I did let him know. I wrote him an eight-page letter just before I went away for a week. In it I described all my grievances and hurts. When I returned, I asked him if he would go see a counselor with me. He said, 'No. What you wrote about us is too personal. After that, I could never go to a counselor.'

"I think it was an excuse, but he continued to use the same reason, and he never changed his mind."

When we asked her why she didn't press her point, she shrugged her shoulders and shook her head. "I don't know. I guess I never really pressed him on anything."

Another woman in the survey described the futility she

felt because all her efforts to change their relationship were dissuaded by her controlling husband. "He always has an excuse that makes him the good guy. Of course, it's always my fault, and that makes me the bad guy. He is oblivious to my needs and desires. They're a joke to him."

Still other women were disappointed by husbands who dismissed their marriage vows.

Unfaithful Husbands

One woman listed her disappointments in this order: 1) mother, 2) father, 3) children, and 4) husband. Then she said, "No, actually my biggest disappointment was my marriage." She went on to explain why. "My trust was undermined by my husband's secret involvements with other women. They had been going on for years before I finally realized it. The proof was there; I just wasn't looking." She gave some of the specific details and then continued. "What hurts the most is, he doesn't think his behavior was that serious. He is totally unaware of how painful his involvements have been for me."

Other times a husband shows genuine sorrow and remorse over his behavior, but that doesn't take away the disappointment that the wife feels. Fran's husband was unfaithful on three occasions over a short period of time. "He said he realized how wrong he was, and he asked me to forgive him. At first I wasn't able to, but after some time, I did forgive him. However, I never acknowledged the anger I was feeling. I just disconnected from my feelings and went on with life.

"Over the years I've become agoraphobic—I'm afraid to go very far from my house, and I have been troubled with feelings of anxiety and panic. When I went to a counselor, I found out there was a connection between my symptoms and my husband's unfaithfulness. Even though it has been years, I am still feeling so much pain." Fran was facing the disappointments she felt for the lost years, the years she carried the pain without resolving it.

Finally women expressed disappointments because more than one marriage didn't work out.

Multiple Husbands, Multiple Disappointments

Several women we surveyed described not just one disappointing marriage, but several. To them, the disappointments weren't just added on top of each other, they were multiplied exponentially. "It's one thing to face the failure of a marriage, but it's quite a different thing to realize you've made the same mistake again, and maybe even again."

Sue, a forty-seven-year-old woman who had been married twice before, was now into the fourth year of her third marriage.

"I took a risk three years ago," she said, "but because of my fiancé's deception during the courtship, I didn't have a clue that it would be so bad. . . . I think my biggest disappointment is that he is so much like both my other husbands. It makes me sick inside. I thought he was so different."

As Sue began to face her disappointment, she also started to understand how her childhood had influenced the selection of her mates. "It all stems back to my dad, who was never there for me when I was a child. I understand now why I have married the type of men I have, but that doesn't resolve my current situation."

A big part of Sue's disappointment is the realization that she will never have what she considers a good marriage.

One thing about the disappointments women experience the second time around: It becomes harder to ignore the harsh truths we need to face about ourselves. Fortunately, many people are finally able to get a healthy handle on what they have done wrong so they can begin to do things differently.

Yet very few of these women had ever told their husbands about their disappointments.

Silence Forces Marital Disappointment to Explode in Anger

Often, a woman's fear of being abandoned by her husband keeps her from telling him about her unhappiness. Instead, she waits until she is so resentful that her anger bursts to the surface, completely out of control. Her emotional outburst begins a deadly back-and-forth cycle.

Dave and Jan know that cycle, just as you probably do. Dave is a laid-back, easygoing kind of guy, a plus in some ways—he doesn't get angry easily, as Jan does. However, he also doesn't carry through on details. That's often a source of disappointment for Jan.

"When the boys were growing up, I saw Dave as the head of the house and the disciplinarian. If one of our teenagers would stay out too late, I'd ask Dave to ground them or take away a privilege."

"I'd hedge on that," Dave admits. "Sometimes I was just too busy. Other times I saw the punishment as a little too stiff. Sometimes I just put it off."

"And that's where the trouble began. By the time Dave got around to punishing Mike, Greg, or Eric it didn't have much effect on them. He just wasn't the strong leader I wanted him to be. I'd finally confront him. And that's when the cycle began. 'Why don't you take care of this issue?' I'd ask."

Dave naturally felt threatened by Jan's explosion, and he responded with anger. "Why me? Why can't you do some of the disciplining?"

An emotional response like this either overpowers the

wife's anger or raises the level of both their anger to a knock-down-drag-out verbal (and maybe even physical) fight.

The argument now focuses on each spouse's defending himself (Jan: "You're supposed to be the head of this house." Dave: "But you're right here when it happens."), rather than talking about how to punish the teenager appropriately.

Later, the husband is left wondering if his wife still loves him. Obviously, it's difficult for her to reassure him of her love at the same time that she is trying to tell him about her hurt. Eventually, she gives up trying, and they reach an unspoken agreement to keep her anger hidden.

Because our relationship with our spouse is so encompassing, and we are so vulnerable in it, we are disappointed in that relationship far more often and more deeply. Someone once said that marriage only provides familiarity; intimacy comes with hard work. Achieving intimacy involves setting aside our unhealthy fantasies about marriage, coming to terms with reality, and becoming comfortable with who we are as well.

A close second to women's disappointment with their husbands and their marriage was disappointment in their relationship with their fathers or mothers or with both parents.

DISAPPOINTMENT #2: FATHERS AND MOTHERS

Many women noted the absence of their fathers in their everyday lives or an ongoing conflict with their mothers. At the root of their disappointment was the feeling that they had never experienced any sense of approval from their parents. One woman expressed it this way: "Neither my mom nor my dad ever told me they loved me. All I ever wanted from them was a simple nod of approval—just to have them say they were proud of me for being an excellent nurse. But no, they gave all their compliments to my brother. I guess. . . ." She did not complete the sentence, perhaps because she became aware that her disappointment went beyond her parents to include other family members as well.

Another woman said, "My dad was always so harsh with me. He yelled at me and never knew how sensitive I really was. I wish I could tell him how he has hurt me. I know now he will never change, but I still long for him to show even a little kindness toward me."

Women grew disappointed because their parents were unavailable, unaccepting, alcoholic, abusive, or dead or divorced. We will look at each type of disappointment individually.

Unavailable Parents

Parents can be present in the home, yet still be unavailable to their children. One woman described her father as a television addict. "I can't remember him ever once reading to me or tucking me into bed. He was always glued to the television. Once I remember going to my dad to ask for help with my homework. He didn't even acknowledge my presence, much less listen to what I was saying. Sometimes he would act like he was listening by nodding his head, but he never stopped and looked at me or responded to my questions. Never!"

Cindy described her mother as emotionally ill, and wrote of the terrible disappointment she felt as a child. "All I can remember about growing up was how crazy Mom always seemed to be. She kept trying to kill herself, especially when I was an adolescent."

Cindy went on to describe how bitter and angry she had been with her mom. "When my mom died this past summer, I realized for the first time that I did love her, and I even felt some compassion for her. But now she's gone, and all my new feelings are mixed up with the old bitterness and anger."

Unaccepting Parents

Laura's response to our questionnaire was typical of so many others; her biggest disappointment was the realization that her mom has never accepted her for who she is. "I've always been a disappointment to my mom, which is really a huge disappointment to me. For instance, she can't accept me because I'm not terribly feminine—I'm rather tomboyish.

"I've learned over the years not to tell Mom too much about my life, and I don't visit her very often. I wish we could be friends, but she has hurt me too often by the critical and unaccepting things she says to me."

Laura's relationship with her mother was echoed over and over again by other women. "I've just become aware," another woman said, "of my disappointment with my mom. She never acknowledged me as a person—my unique ability to think and do things. I've been compliant up until recently. Now I simply avoid her. I don't have much trust in my own ability because I didn't get a lot of affirmation as a person or encouragement to do things. I'm just beginning to deal with this hurt."

Women also talked about their disappointment with alcoholic or abusive parents.

Alcoholic Parents

We are probably more aware of the losses experienced by a child who grows up in an alcoholic family than ever before. Yet we rarely hear of the longing an adult child still has for a relationship with that alcoholic parent. "My biggest disappointment," one woman wrote, "is not knowing my father because of his alcoholism."

Another woman, Connie, described all the broken promises her parents made to her, many of them significant ones, like the time her father admitted himself into an alcoholism treatment program as a result of a family intervention. "I couldn't believe it when he started drinking again the day he got out of the program. Ever since that day, I've been estranged from my dad and mom and two of my three siblings. I guess that speaks volumes about my disappointment and hurt."

Broken promises were a recurring theme among adult children of alcoholics. Those repeatedly broken promises added up to major losses and hurts, many of which were hidden because they were so extremely painful. It's almost as if women raised in alcoholic homes feel so much pain when they look back at their families that they have a greater investment in keeping their dreams and fantasies alive. For them, the truth just hurts too much.

Often alcoholic parents are also abusive parents (but not all abusive parents are alcoholics).

Abusive Parents

It's difficult to understand how our hope can stay alive so long under cruel conditions. Chris, the oldest of two daughters, described her father as a "rageaholic." "Dad would clobber me, kick me, and pull my hair. He did that regularly until I was nineteen. He would often beat my mother as well. I have a very vivid memory of him beating her with the back side of a silver mirror he had given her. He hit her so hard he bent the handle!

"My mom was once very pretty, but she became an overeater soon after they got married. My dad would call her ugly nicknames because of her weight, and he didn't seem to care who was around. The strange thing is, even though my dad never beat my younger sister, she became a compulsive eater like my mom."

Chris was very aware of the hurt caused by her father, yet when we asked about the biggest disappointment in her life, she said, "That's easy: never being able to win my dad's approval or love—or even feel that he liked me."

Chris was forty-three years old when we talked with her. We asked her what her father was like now. "He visits us twice a year," she said, "when he's talking to us. If anyone in my family does something he doesn't approve of, however, we get the silent treatment. He hasn't talked to me now for almost two years because my daughter did something that he didn't like. I guess the only thing that's different now is that he doesn't hit me or my mom, but the silent treatment still hurts."

Finally, women were disappointed because of a parent's death or divorce.

Parents' Divorce or Deaths

Many adults are still struggling with their own parents' divorce. Usually their disappointments are related to the absence of one parent, often the father, and also to the loss of a healthy model of marriage to pattern their own lives after. A part of nearly every child's response to his or her parents' divorce is to assume responsibility for what happened between Mom and Dad and then feel guilty for not being able to hold them together. It's frightening how many women have repeated their parents' situation, despite their disappointment about the end of their parents' marriage. One woman wrote, "My father left my mother for another woman." Later in the questionnaire she revealed another disappointment. "My husband—who is an alcoholic—left me to live with another woman."

Other women were disappointed when they felt abandoned by a parent who died. "As I get further along in my recovery," Meryl wrote, "I'm realizing that things always get back to my mother, and the fact that I didn't ever really bond with her.

"She had cancer all of my childhood," this woman explained, "but it never showed. . . . She died when I was thirteen, and at the time, I didn't feel anything. I didn't even miss her. When I did start to feel, there was no place for me to go, since my dad was a critical, self-made man, and my brother resented me. I felt abandoned then, and I still feel abandoned now, even in relation to my own husband and children. I'm just discovering the powerful impact all that had on my ability to be emotionally intimate and to trust someone's love, even the love of my own daughters."

Whether it is due to death or divorce, the women we surveyed often felt deep loss because one of their parents was absent. Many times the father was missing. We think that fathers don't have much of an impact on their children. Perhaps the best proof to the contrary is the longing expressed by women who lost their father when they were children, either through death or divorce. (For additional information on the role of the father, we suggest that you read Dave's book *Making Peace with Your Father*.)

Kim's father left her mother when Kim was just nine years old. She remembers trying to call him on the phone, and not being able to find him. When she finally did talk to him, he told her never to call him again. That vivid memory, that rejection, still burns within her.

Not long after her phone conversation with her father, Kim's mother was hospitalized, and Kim was put into one foster home after another. Kim naturally felt abandoned.

Today Kim struggles with both anorexia and bulimia as well as feelings of worthlessness. The one thing Kim can't come to terms with, even as an adult, is that no one understood why it hurt her so much when her dad told her never to contact him again.

The women who answered our questionnaire ranged in age from their early twenties to their sixties and seventies, and those who said they were disappointed by their parents covered the entire gamut. In fact, some of the older women noted their age and commented, "Even at my age, I am still struggling with my unrealized hopes and expectations about my parents."

Women were disappointed with their marriages and their husbands, with their parents, and finally with themselves.

DISAPPOINTMENT #3: MYSELF

The third most common response was, "My biggest disappointment is me!" This disappointment was usually connected to other disappointments—disapproval from their parents, lack of interest from their husbands, difficulties in raising their children. Many felt responsible for these disappointments.

"I could have done something differently," some wrote. "If I had tried harder, things might have been different." If their kids were having problems, many women felt they were to blame. One woman wrote, "My kids are messing up their lives, I'm a wreck, and my husband is always angry at me. I was not prepared for this. I am literally falling apart. I am so disappointed with myself. I know it's all because of me—I have been so weak and out-of-control. I've failed miserably."

Regardless of what we are disappointed about, the pendulum eventually swings over to being disappointed in ourselves. Sometimes we see the connection between our disappointment in ourselves and our disappointment in others, but that connection usually remains unnoticed, and we struggle with the two disappointments as separate and distinct issues. What things do women struggle with most within themselves? The women we surveyed expressed six common themes.

1. "Something Is Wrong with Me."

Sometimes there was an objective basis for the women's disappointment with themselves. For example, several women were disappointed in themselves because they had chronic diseases, such as diabetes, or learning disorders, such as dyslexia, which still affected them as adults. Yet most women were disappointed by something subjective— their view of their childhood, or of themselves, for instance—that could not be accurately evaluated.

In her book *Unrealistic Expectations,* Barbra Minar wrote, "One place we begin collecting unrealistic standards is our family of origin. The way we interpret what went on between ourselves and family members is the key. The old tapes echoing in our minds color our expectations of ourselves." [2]

We carry these colored expectations into our adult lives. Women who were perfectionistic often said they were disappointed in "my own imperfections." Becky's struggle with self-acceptance spilled over into all her relationships because she applied the same perfectionistic standards to others. "I find I'm not only disappointed in myself, but in my family and, quite often, with people in general," she told us. "I sometimes wonder if I'll ever be able to accept the inevitability of human beings always messing up."

Other women shared how they struggled with constant negative thoughts about themselves, especially when they were alone. Vera told about her forty-year struggle with "a very poor sense of self." She said, "I've always felt powerless and unable to get myself together. On top of that, I've struggled with feeling that no one really knows me—the deep down inside me. Part of me longs to be known by someone else, but of course, another part of me is terrified at the thought. Who could ever accept me if they knew that deep down inside part of me?" Thankfully, Vera just couldn't bring herself to accept the fact that she was as bad on the inside as she feared. That refusal was her source of hope.

Still other women described their disappointment in themselves as a feeling of emptiness, like "a hole that can't be touched or filled." Betty Friedan, a founder of the women's movement, was among the first to talk about this hole. "Each suburban wife struggled with it alone," she said. "As she made the beds, shopped for groceries, matched slipcover material, ate peanut butter sandwiches with her children, chauffeured Cub Scouts and Brownies, lay beside her husband at night—she was afraid to ask even of herself the silent question—'Is this all?'"[3]

Some women talked about plans they had made and not followed through on, or training they had completed for a career that they had not pursued. Now, years later, they looked back and blamed themselves for not doing something that had been so important to them at the time.

2. "There's Immorality in My Past."

An immoral past was the basis for some women's disappointment in themselves. Sheila described herself as "a rebellious teenager." "I got into drugs at the beginning of high school and ended up never doing any of the things I had looked forward to doing. I lost my virginity. I hated my parents and their constant attempts to help me during that time. I still fight a rebelliousness within myself that I don't understand. I still struggle with the feeling that my life lacks character." Sheila feels these disappointments so deeply that she even compares herself to one of her children, whom she believes has genuine character, and uses that comparison to remind herself of her faults.

Another woman echoed Sheila's struggle because of things she did when she was younger. She used drugs, acted out sexually, and "did a lot of crazy things." In her marriage, she described herself as "the abuser." She said, "I have abused my husband, both verbally and physically. I've done everything to him I said I would never do. Now he wants a divorce. I turned out just like my father, whom I've hated all my life. I am so disappointed in myself."

3. "I Had an Abortion."

Several women talked about abortions they had when they were younger. Many of them said that they had not been fully aware of the consequences of what they were doing and that they had been reacting to pressure from their parents or a boyfriend. Later, they ended up blaming themselves, not only for ending a pregnancy, but for getting pregnant in the first place.

One woman said she had been in therapy for several years and still struggled with the abortion she had when she was first married. "There was very little being said about abortion when my husband and I decided we couldn't afford to have a child yet. The courts had just legalized abortion, and even the doctor agreed it was probably the best thing to do." She went on to say, "I am filled with guilt and remorse everytime there is something in the news about abortion protests or court intervention. . . . I hate myself for what I did. I simply can't forgive myself, and I can never forget. My husband gets angry with me and says I am belaboring something that has already happened, but he just doesn't understand what that experience did to me."

Another woman said, "I am so disappointed in myself because I had an abortion. I will never forgive myself for that! I had a choice and I made the wrong one. How does one ever get over that kind of disappointment?"

4. "I Struggle with My Weight [or Appearance]."

One of the ways women often cope with disappointment is to overeat. The result is additional disappointments, especially in terms of body image. "It permeates every aspect of my life," one woman said. "I've allowed it to be a source of shame and pain. I use it to avoid men and social situations in general. I'm not even that heavy (about 15 pounds over normal weight for my height), but I have allowed my weight to severely limit me."

Other women said they were disappointed in themselves because they couldn't get control of their eating. Some commented on the vicious cycle they were caught in. "I'm disappointed about something, so I eat. Then I get angry at myself for eating, and I feel more disappointed in myself, which causes me to eat more. Sometimes I take out my anger on my husband or my kids. Eventually I get totally depressed."

Weight problems are often tied to hurts within the family. One woman said, "My biggest disappointment is me. I'm overweight, and my whole family puts me down for it. I have tried to lose weight, but nothing ever works. I'm at the point where I am embarrassed to even go out anywhere."

5. "I Have No Direction." "I Never Finish Anything."

In many cases, women's expectations were so high they couldn't possibly reach them, and now they realized that. In other cases, their dreams were realistic, but they had been set aside for valid reasons. Now they looked back upon them with sadness and a sense of personal loss.

Several women were disappointed in themselves for their failure to complete college. One woman had been trying for over ten years. Another woman said, "I haven't finished college because I seldom complete any of the classes I've taken. I've only completed four classes in the past seven years. I'm a professional procrastinator. I also have a problem with rage. I often wonder if the procrastination and the rage are connected."

Another woman who failed to complete college said she struggles with fear. "If I actually made the effort to attend classes, I think I would flunk out." Even though she was valedictorian of her high school class and was offered eight four-year scholarships, she is paralyzed by her fear of failure.

One woman was disappointed in herself because she had to take the graduate school admission exam three times before she passed. She was disappointed by her inability to achieve her goals in what she considered a realistic time frame.

Other women were struggling with themselves because they felt their lives were aimless—they had no goals or direction. They described themselves as procrastinating, struggling with parental expectations, and staying in relationships that were counter to their own desires and objectives. One woman said, "My biggest disappointment is that I'm not secure and confident enough to experience more of life. I settle for too little."

Some women are afraid to venture out beyond the safety of the known. "I am ever fearful of being 'found out,'" the woman said of herself, "and discarded." At the end of her sentence she drew a sad face with tears.

Teddy Roosevelt called those who settle for too little "poor spirits who neither enjoy much nor suffer much because they live in the gray twilight that knows neither victory nor defeat." That's a good description of how these women felt.

6. *"I Have No Security."*

Many women described their disappointment with themselves in terms of their lack of security, especially financial security. Their struggle is summed up in one woman's description: "I have never had financial stability. I always thought my husband would provide this, but he hasn't, and I don't feel capable of providing it. I find myself daydreaming of how it would be if I had financial stability—not financial abundance, just stability."

Some of these women's financial problems were caused by a divorce and an ex-husband's refusal to make the alimony payments. One woman's problems were caused by a husband's suicide and the resulting financial chaos. Another woman told of a husband who lied about money and lost everything in a business venture. In each case, the woman described herself as working as hard as she could to change the situation, but only "ending up being further behind."

Disappointment in husbands and marriages, in parents, and in themselves were the three major disappointments women expressed in our survey. But five others were also significant; we'll talk about those in the next chapter. Again, these disappointments may sound very familiar. By listening to these women, you will uncover some of your own disappointments, the first step in the process of saying goodbye to them.

—3—

What Else Do Women Want?

I know all about disappointments," Carole told us. "I never expected to get through life without some problems and pain, but I sure didn't think they would all come down on me at once. And I never thought I would have to face them alone."

Carole's family was on vacation when their neighborhood was devastated by a wildfire that swept down from the mountains, consuming everything in its path. Everything they owned was lost, even the dog and cat that had been a part of their family for so many years. And because Carole's business was at home, the family also lost a good portion of its income.

In the months after the fire, Carole became more and more concerned with the deteriorating health of her husband, Rich. When the diagnosis came, it was worse than she could have imagined: Rich's neurological condition, which affected him both physically and mentally, was progressive and relentlessly deteriorating. He had Huntington's Disease, which is like having Multiple Sclerosis, Alzheimer's, and Tourette's Syndrome (in which the patient grunts, groans, barks, and swears uncontrollably) all at one time. There was no cure and there was no treatment.

"I had a house to build and furnish, endless insurance companies to deal with, a hopeless financial situation dropped into my lap, and a husband who was becoming more helpless by the day. After a short time, the friends who had rallied around to help went back to their own lives, and I was left to cope alone. I tried to pray, but it was hard to approach God when He no longer seemed to be listening. Disappointments? Oh, yes, I know all about them!"

Women's disappointments come in many varieties and intensities. In this chapter, we will look at five other major disappointments women mentioned again and again.

"IT'S MY KIDS."

"My children are my major disappointments in life," said Pat. She told of her abusive husband and how she withdrew from him emotionally and directed all her attention to their three children. Today Pat struggles with the way her now-adult children treat her. "No matter what I do for them," she explained, "they just don't love me the way I need them to. I gave my kids everything, but they let me down."

Women who find their marriage relationships empty often do just what Pat did: They transfer their dreams to their children. But those who look to their children to fulfill their dreams usually end up with a double dose of disappointment. In her book *Unrealistic Expectations*, Barbara Minar says, "If we control things right, we can try to create everlasting happiness between mother and child. We find, however, even though we have treasured, happy moments, we are out of control. Did our baby forget to bring our ticket to Happiness Land?"[1]

When Pat described her son's actions toward her, she said, "His attitude is very similar to his father's, and he treats me just like my husband did. He can be so abusive, and just plain rude." Of her daughters, she said, "It seems they try to avoid me." Struggling to hold back tears, she told us of the overwhelming emptiness she felt inside. "I always thought that once I had a family, my husband would fill some of that emptiness and my children would fill in the rest. I guess I just expected too much from them."

Jean wrote on her questionnaire: "My biggest disappointment is the choices of my children and that I have failed to make a difference in their lives. They were hurt by their father's and my divorce, and we waged a custody battle that went on for five years. When it was finally over, I was convinced my love for the children would make everything okay for them. It didn't. I feel so guilty and helpless I can hardly stand it."

Some women described the heartbreak of watching helplessly as their children struggled with drugs. Others told of kids who were alcoholics, or who had married alcoholics. Several mothers related their incredible pain and disappointment at discovering that one of their kids had AIDS. And a common thread ran through every one of these stories: a profound sense of helplessness.

While children can be one of the greatest joys in a woman's life, they can also be a source of real pain and disappointment.

Women were also disappointed by men in general, not just by their husbands.

"ALL MEN ARE DISAPPOINTING."

A number of women noted their disappointment in men. One woman put it this way: "Men pretend to be one thing and later you find out they are really something quite different. They're all phonies." Said another, "There is such a lack of good men. There just aren't any around who are trustworthy and godly. I haven't found anyone I want to invest my life in and build a relationship with."

Dorothy told us about her particular disappointment. "When I was in my twenties, I had a boyfriend I loved totally and completely," she said. "After we had been dating for three years, he broke off our relationship to go back to an old girlfriend, and within two months they were married. I was devastated! I couldn't turn off my love for him. Eventually I married someone else, but for years, whenever I made love with my husband I wished I was with my old boyfriend. Every time, I would break down and cry. My husband never understood why, and I didn't have the heart to tell him. Finally, after about fifteen years, I was able to let go of my old boyfriend. But I still have times when I wish I could have married him."

Those who had been through a divorce and had never remarried talked of their loneliness.

"When my husband left, my self-image was destroyed and caused me to withdraw from life," Marjorie told us. "I've learned to live alone and to be self-sufficient, but I'm not able to trust anyone. After twelve years of being single again, and after having had many surface relationships, there is no significant person in my life. Even though there were bad times with my husband, and even though I know I was mentally abused and controlled by him, I still tear up when I remember the good times we had. It's when I think of those happy memories that I can't stand my loneliness, and I feel so deeply disappointed in my life."

Loneliness was also a common refrain among women who had never married, and they voiced that as a major disappointment.

"I'VE NEVER MARRIED." "I'VE NEVER HAD CHILDREN."

One by one, each of Ellen's friends married and had children. As Ellen watched from the sidelines, she became more and more acutely aware of one of life's bigger disappointments—the ticking of her biological clock. Ellen is not alone. We heard this scenario again and again from women who had never married. "God has given other women mates, but He hasn't given me anyone," said one almost-middle-aged woman sadly. "He could have if He wanted to, but He hasn't. The problem is either me or that God didn't provide for me."

Several women talked about special men with whom they had fallen in love, yet for one reason or another, they didn't marry. "I let a really good one get away," one woman said. "I know he's a good one because I know his present wife and family. I sometimes look at her and think to myself, *That should be me.* But I can't blame anyone but myself. I'm the one who broke it off because I had other plans at the time. Little did I know that fifteen years later I'd still be single."

Other women focused more on their childlessness. "Somehow, I feel my childlessness is an inadequacy within myself," one lady told us. "It's an emptiness deep within me." Said another, "I'm forty-three, but I look thirty-two. I'm not married and never have been, and I haven't had children. I'm thinking now that I may never get married and have kids. But I can't get over my desire to be a mother. I am really grieving over this one!"

Many women mentioned their deep disappointment over their infertility and the exhausting process of trying to get pregnant; closely related are disappointments of miscarriages. The inability to have a child or the difficulty of carrying a child to full term are unique disappointments shared by many. Although they are married, these women, too, share the emptiness that single women describe.

Sometimes, one loss brings on yet another. Women also told of broken friendships.

"I'VE LOST MY FRIENDS."

It's not unusual for loneliness to accompany other disappointments. "I understand that my friends all have lives of their own," Carole said, "but there are times when I need them so much. In the year after the fire, my daughter was married and my son left for college. Both live across the country from me. I'm glad the kids are going on with their lives, but I have to admit that I feel terribly alone. My husband really isn't able to go out much any more, and I work at home. My friends just aren't here when I need them."

Many times, women who have endured a broken marriage relationship experience the added burden of seeing their friendships weaken or break apart. "After the disappointment of a failed marriage, I have to struggle with the abandonment I feel from my friends," one hurting woman wrote. "They all seem to have disappeared. Now I have to adjust to a roommate, and I'm having a really difficult time."

Dee talked about the painful loneliness she has endured since her divorce. "I can't think of one friend who I can honestly say has shown any interest in me or in my life. Nobody seems to follow through on the things they say they'll do. When I was going through my divorce, I realized I didn't have anyone I felt was really there for me."

Another woman summed up her own feelings this way: "My biggest disappointment is with people. I try hard to be a good friend to others, but I keep walking away feeling used. When you are good to other people, they are never good back."

When everyone else has left you, at least you still have God. . . . Don't you? Some women felt otherwise.

"EVEN GOD HAS LET ME DOWN."

"God has always been an important part of my life and of my family's life," said Carole. "I'm not perfect, not by any means, but I have to say I have strived to follow God and do things His way. So here's my question: If I have done everything right to the best of my ability, why is God letting so much go wrong for me?"

Carole's is an age-old question, one many of us are called upon to wrestle with. When we have done everything right, does God owe us something in return? Many women told us they certainly thought so. And when the expected payback didn't come, their disappointment was profound.

Grace said, "My fiancé and I did it God's way. We thought if we followed what God said about sex, He would bless us with a good sex life. But right from the beginning, our sex life has been horrible. I'm disappointed that we struggled so hard to do what was right and got nothing in return."

"I've done it both ways," Emily said. "I've held the line with some men and refused to go to bed with them, and I've given in to others and slept with them. Either way, I end up the loser. I'm pushing forty and still single. I just don't think God cares, at least not about me."

As we listened to Carole and Grace and Emily (and so many others) talk about the dashing of their hopes and dreams "in spite of doing everything right," we could feel the anger churning beneath their disappointments. When we suggested, "It sounds as though you're angry with God," almost every woman insisted that was not so. "It's not that I'm angry," Carole said, "it's just that I want to know why. I want to understand." Women like Carole weren't able to hide their anger, but neither were they able to admit it—not to themselves, not to us, and not to God.

For some women, the disappointment related to God's failure to answer important prayers in their lives the way they thought He should have answered them. These prayers weren't just for a boost up the ladder of success, either, or even for such matters as the healing of loved ones. Many of the women talked about asking God for guidance in making important decisions in their lives. And at the time they believed God had given them guidance. Later, though, they felt those decisions had been major mistakes.

"I had a great job," one woman said. "I loved my work and I was good at it. The people I worked for appreciated me and affirmed me constantly for my accomplishments, and I was fulfilled in what I was doing. But I had this nagging feeling that it wasn't enough, that I needed to be doing something more meaningful. I felt I needed to be working in a ministry. When an opportunity came along, I quit my job and went to work for an organization where I could serve God." The outcome? "I've never been more miserable in my life. Either God wanted me to be miserable, or I haven't got a clue about how to figure out what He wants me to do." It can sometimes be extremely difficult to distinguish between what we want and what God wants. As Lee Ezell asks in *The Cinderella Syndrome,* "What is it I am really longing for? How does what I want line up with what God wants for me?"[2] This can be a very hard question to answer. Without the counsel and insights of others, it may be impossible.

The problem is multiplied because so many of our ideas about God, and what we can and should expect of Him, are based on faulty teaching from our childhood. Too often we haven't taken the time to study the Scriptures and learn the truth of who God is and what kind of relationship we can have with Him. To take this step requires that we wake up and face reality, even though it is so much more comfortable to cling to our dreams and to blame someone else.

"More and more, I'm learning to take a broader view of my disappointments," Carole said. "The bottom-line truth is that life is full of disappointments. None of us is going to avoid them." Carole is right. And our human tendency is to look for the easiest possible way out. We grasp for a temporary "Band-aid" solution, anything that will help us feel better for the moment. But if we are to triumph, we need to face our disappointments straight on and then work toward discovering new ways of handling them.

"In every situation, we do have options," said Carole. "It's up to us to search them out and do what we can do." In an effort to do just that, she has taken a careful look at her disappointments and expectations. She is discarding her old coping methods that have failed to work, and she is trying new ones: She has joined a support group with other caregivers, she is taking the initiative in reaching out to friends, and she is re-examining her ideas of God and how He deals with His children. (We'll talk about how each of us can make changes like these in coming chapters.)

By now, you are thinking about the various disappointments in your own life. Good for you. Here are some reflections to help you determine the coping approaches you might take with them.

Personal Reflections:
Your Own Disappointments

1. *Think about the disappointments in your life. How would you complete the following statements?*

I have been disappointed about:

a. _____

b. _____

c. _____

d. _____

What I expected in each case was:

a. _____

b. _____

c. _____

d. _____

2. *Now look back at the disappointments you listed. In each one, can you identify the person who frustrated, hurt, or injured you? Write down that person's name.*

_____ *frustrated me.*

_____ *hurt me.*

_____ *injured me.*

3. Is there a particular disappointment in your life that you just can't seem to get over? Describe it as thoroughly as you can. _____

_____

_____

What I expected was _____

_____

_____

I am disappointed in myself because _____

_____

_____

What I expected of myself was _____

_____

_____

Most of our disappointments come from the dreams we have for our lives and the expectations we set for ourselves. In the next chapter we will look at those dreams and where they come from.

—4—

What Are Our Dreams?

I t's beautiful," Jan yelled down the stairs to Dave. "Wait till you see the huge bedrooms . . . and the view from up here is incredible!"

Dave hadn't gotten to the upstairs part of the house yet, but he was getting the picture—Jan was sure this was the house for them, and she had already started to plan how they could purchase it. The boys were running all over exploring every nook and cranny, and Jan was becoming more and more enthused by the minute. It was a huge, old two-story Colonial with white pillars out front, set on an acre and a third of land, with a pool in the back and a fence around the entire parklike property. Jan couldn't understand why Dave couldn't see all the possibilities she was seeing in this house.

"We don't want this monstrosity of a house," Dave said. "The upkeep will eat us alive. The pool is green with algae, the cleanup will cost a fortune, and there must be thirty trees in the front yard. Who's going to trim all those trees and rake all those leaves? Not only that, we'd need a tractor to get the lawn mowed."

As they stood talking in the quaint butler's pantry, Jan had an answer for every objection Dave raised. "We'll find a way," she repeated over and over.

Jan saw a look of resignation cross Dave's face as he realized that the boys and she were already moving in.

Neither of them had noticed the brown nicotine stains covering the windows and the woodwork. That discovery would come later. They also neglected to inquire about the plumbing and the electrical systems, but none of that information would have mattered anyway—Jan was home!

Dave and Jan bought that house and lived there for over three years. "We still marvel at how we put up with the gophers, the six toilets that always were in need of repair, a septic tank that overflowed, especially when we had company, and the ongoing battle with the green water in the pool. We survived it, but it put great stress on us and on our family," Jan said. "What neither of us realized at the time was that we were dealing with something more, much more, than buying a house."

Another factor was at work, a hidden driving force motivating Jan to press right ahead in spite of the warning signals to wait and evaluate the purchase. She was faced with an opportunity to fulfill an important dream; the house was similar to one she had dreamed about as a child.

THE DREAM TELLS THE STORY OF THE DREAMER

Our dreams are the bright side of our disappointments. The English poet William Wordsworth wrote in 1807:

> There was a time when meadow, grove, and stream;
> The earth, and every common sight;
> To me did seem apparelled in celestial light;
> The glory and the freshness of a dream.

Childhood dreams are like that, glorious and fresh—refreshing because they are not necessarily the same as the dreams our mothers and fathers had for us, even though their dreams for us (and for themselves) may have helped shape our dream. Neither are they necessarily what we thought we could realistically be or do. Instead, they are the essence of what we wish we could be or what we wish we could have out of life. They served us well. They allowed us to do anything we wanted to do and be anything we wanted to be. They provided us with a way to achieve a happily-ever-after ending.

Yet dreaming is not always looked upon favorably. Dictionaries even define the dreamer as an impractical and unrealistic person. Many of us were told as a child to "Stop being such a dreamer" or that "Wishing won't make it happen." Adults may not have said it directly, but we interpreted the message as, "It's wrong to dream."

Our parents were probably given the same warning by their own parents, so they concluded early in life (just as we did) that dreams and wishes were frivolous and without much value.

How could any of us have known how important our dreams were in the development of our sense of self?

Dr. James P. Comer, M.D., a professor of child psychiatry at Yale University's Child Study Center, says, "Most of us have hopes and dreams for the future. But we often think of the stated hopes of young people as kid stuff that will go away or change a thousand times before adulthood. Some will change and some will not, but all are important. A dream is a goal that helps give a young person direction, purpose, and organization."[1]

Even though our dreams are seemingly forgotten, hidden from our awareness, they often shape our experiences as we live day to day, forming our expectations and surprising us with the intensity of their power to influence decisions, such as the spouse we choose or the house we buy. Our dreams can cause us to jump into things—and to pressure ourselves and others—as we seek to fulfill them. ("Every time I feel I *have* to have something—or do something—I remember those six toilets that were always in need of repair," Jan says.)

Edmond Rostand, a French playwright, said it well: "The dream, alone, is of interest. What is life, without a dream?"[2]

Dreams tell our story. They are as individual and unique as our personalities. As we attach meaning and significance to them, dreams draw us into the future, giving hope for all that may yet be. But where did those early dreams come from, and what do they tell us about ourselves?

If we look at our dreams seriously, we will find some clues to the parts of us that have been wounded and need to be healed or to the parts of us that have been neglected yet are so worthy of recognition.

The Source of Our Dreams

All children have dreams. For some of us, our imaginations took off in every direction. We not only dreamed about what it might be like to be a dancer, a doctor, or a mommy, but we expanded our dreams to include other aspects of life, like a large house with white pillars out front and a rolling green lawn. Sometimes our childhood dreams were related to someone special, such as a neighbor, cousin, or grandparent; or to a special object, such as a doll or music box or treehouse, that represented an important value or need in our lives as children.

Sometimes, early hurts and frustrations added detail as well as determination to our dreams.

Early Hurts and Frustrations

One woman told us, "When my mom canceled a long-anticipated outing for some unknown reason, which didn't make sense to me, I told myself, 'When I become a mom, I'll always do what I said I was going to do. I'll never disappoint my own kids like that.'"

Another said, "Every time my mother spanked me, I told myself that this would never happen again. I determined I would always be a good girl and that when I became an adult, I would make sure people treated me kindly."

Our expectations begin the moment we leave the non-disappointing womb and enter the disappointing world. It's a setup. We experienced a perfect womb, so we expect a perfect world. The disappointments that follow, even in early childhood, shape our hopes and dreams for the future.

One woman told us how her dad often lost control of his temper. "When I was little, he would scream at me as he hit me. I was terrified. As I lay on my bed crying, I remember telling myself things like 'I'll never marry a man like him! The man I marry will be kind and gentle. And if he ever yells and hits me like that, I'll make him stop. I wouldn't let him treat my children like this!'" When we experience disappointment as a child, we determine that things will be different when we grow up.

Our dreams can be shaped by a hurt as small as a broken toy or a harsh word or by the incidence of traumatic abuse. Whether small or large, the disappointments of childhood have a powerful influence on what we dream.

Childhood Abuse

Women whose childhood was chaotic or lonely or painful often escaped into their own private dream world where everything was pleasant and peaceful. One friend told us, "My dream was of a peaceful reality. I imagined that everything was okay, even when everyone in my family was yelling at each other. In my dream, none of it was happening. I looked at my dolls during those times, and saw how peaceful they were. I wanted to be like them, just sitting there, never having to see or hear the screaming. So I created a world like theirs for myself. No violence or yelling—only peace."

Another woman told us she remembered lying on her bed as a child and escaping an abusive parent by traveling to some distant land of long ago. "I imagined myself as the princess who married the prince and lived happily ever after. Or I dreamed I was an elegant lady who lived in the beautiful, big house down the street."

Some women told of burying themselves in a romantic novel as many teenagers do. One woman said, "I imagined myself as one of the characters, pretending that what I was reading was my 'real life.' What was happening at that moment in our house was the story. I told myself soon I would be rescued by a man, my prince, who is the hero of the story." Several women said, "I still use romantic novels to escape now."

Sometimes the traumas of our early lives were so painful that we simply stopped dreaming and focused instead on surviving. We carry this survival mode of living into adulthood. Abused children don't have the time or energy to escape within their minds; they need to watch carefully what is going on around them so they can protect themselves. This pattern can start early, especially when traumatic events are repeated over and over again and become a way of life for the child.

Yet women who were raised without extreme trauma also were led to dream dreams.

Exaggerated Expectations

Women who were raised in emotionally healthy homes had more time to dream even bigger dreams—possibly impossible dreams—of what adulthood would be like. Positive childhood experiences sometimes teach us that "The sky is the limit," and that our limitation is the scope of our imagination. The charming and believable Jiminy Cricket assures us that the theme song of Pinocchio is true: "When you wish upon a star, your dreams come true." So we dream we can meet any challenge and succeed at any task.

One woman said, "My father always read to me and my brothers. He always chose the most interesting books, with stories of high adventure and intrigue. I think my childhood dreams were formed in part out of that delightful time with my father. I dreamed I would someday see the world, and actually have seen a big part of it."

Childhood dreams shape the expectations we all bring with us to adulthood, but we all came to them in our own way. The brother of the woman whose father read those exciting stories could have formed a completely different dream from listening to them. The personal experiences of our childhood affect us each uniquely and thus shape individual dreams.

REMEMBERING OUR DREAMS

As we talked to women, we asked them to remember their dreams—those that had come true, and those that had not. Some women could remember dreams easily, while for others it took some time. It seemed that their dreams had been crowded out by the fast pace of their lives, by worry about their futures, and by their frustrations about today.

Jan found she had to make an effort to remember her dreams too, but once she began to allow them to seep back into her thoughts, she was surprised; it was like opening a floodgate to images she had not thought of for years, dreams that had been long forgotten.

"I realized my early dreams had everything to do with how I viewed myself and life today, and I discovered parts of me that were expressed in my dreams that I had never seen before. The dreams became like an unfolding story about who I am deep down inside, a person quite a bit different from the person I show to the world.

"I listed the dreams, hopes, and expectations I had and still have, pages and pages of them. The first dream: I wanted to be a professional ice skater. Remembering that dream startled me a bit. I hadn't thought of it since I was probably five years old. Next came an aspiration to be a well-known tennis player. Then a dream about being a dancer. I also wrote that I wanted to be an accomplished musician or maybe a famous artist.

"Next came images of places I dreamed I would live. You guessed it: At the top of that list was a huge two-story white Colonial house with pillars in the front and a wide veranda. I remembered walking by a house like that every day on my way to elementary school. My house would have a porch with comfortable rocking chairs in which my friends could sit and have tea with me and look out at the beautiful trees and flowers surrounding us. The inside of the house would have a huge entry hall with a long winding staircase, a perfect place for weddings and other get-togethers.

"But the most important part of the house would be the 'morning room,' a bright breakfast room with skylights and French doors leading out to a brick patio (we do have French doors leading to a brick patio in our present home, but no breakfast room with skylights). Here one could sit and read or look out at the lush green surroundings and feel the cheerfulness and warmth of the sunshine.

"Another important part of my dream was a menagerie of dogs and horses and cats with their litters of kittens, and other animals that would roam over the peaceful grounds. When I shared this dream with Dave, he listened intently and then asked sheepishly, 'Is there any way you could do the dream without all those animals?'

"Of course, the family in my dream was perfect, playing games peacefully together and always happy to be there at the house. In the evening we would sit around the dinner table and laugh and listen to everyone talk about their day. Meals would be special, memorable times, when we would hold hands and pray together. I pictured my husband sitting at the head of the table, leading the family in meaningful discussions and reading to us from the Bible. Decorations, food, and meaningful traditions would abound during holidays.

"I also dreamed I would be a perfect mother, cheerfully loading the kids into my Jeep Cherokee (a contemporary adaptation), the dogs in the back seat, for a trip to the grocery store or a fun outing. At the same time I would be the perfect wife who was so well organized she could juggle taking care of the kids, housework, gourmet cooking, and a career. I would take walks in the woods, have time to read novels, and teach my girls (!) to sew (as you probably know by now, we had three boys). And so the list went on."

We suggest that you take time now for this type of personal reflection, which Jan found to be so beneficial when she was saying goodbye to her disappointments.

Personal Reflections:
The Story of Your Dreams

Maybe you dreamed of being a great musician, a photojournalist, a famous ballerina, or a brain surgeon. Or maybe your dream is similar to that of a friend of ours, who dreamed she would do commercials on TV someday. Or similar to that of another friend, who dreamed she would become a famous children's book author.

What are your dreams? Write down as many of your dreams as you can remember. Go into as much detail as possible. The more dreams you come up with, the more information you will have to work with throughout the remainder of this book. Remember that some dreams will be about things you may never expect to achieve today. Put them down anyway. Remember, dreams tell a fascinating story about who you are.

When Jan was doing this exercise, she found it very helpful to talk into a tape recorder when she was alone. Later, as she listened to the tape, she was surprised to hear so much emotion in her voice, much more than she had allowed herself to admit at the time.

What if you feel like one woman we talked to, who said she didn't have any dreams? "I gave them all up a long time ago, when I got married," she told us. "In fact, when you asked me about my dreams, the very idea seemed foreign to me. My life is purely about other people. My husband and my kids have taken my dreams away from me. They are gone!"

If you identify with this woman, you may have a

hard time getting started, but know that your dreams are somewhere inside you just the same, hidden beneath your disappointments. We encourage you to start by writing down just one dream. That dream will trigger others, and you may be surprised by what dreams you discover.

Here are some ideas to get your thinking started. What dreams and expectations did you have (or still have) about:

1. The kind of person you would be. (Maybe you dreamed you would someday have a wonderful marriage to a perfect man, have tons of kids, and live in the suburbs.)

_____

_____

_____

2. The man you wanted to marry. (Maybe you wanted to marry a doctor because your father was one. Or you wanted to marry a man who would be kind and loving to you and your children. Or a man who would be very strong, making decisions for the family and providing you and your children with all the niceties of life.)

_____

_____

_____

3. *The house you wanted to live in. (Maybe you dreamed, or still dream, of a place where you would live—a tiny hideaway in the French countryside, a place on the Gulf in Florida, a cabin on a peaceful lake, or maybe a river houseboat.)*

_____

_____

_____

4. *Your children. How many children did you want, and what did you think they would be like? (Maybe you dreamed that your children would be perfectly adjusted and loved and would turn out to be famous doctors, missionary pilots, ministers, or scientists.)*

_____

_____

_____

5. *Your marriage. (Maybe your dream was to be loved unconditionally for who you are, and the perfect marriage meant that your husband would love you that way. Maybe your dream was that your mate would always want the same things for your marriage as you did and would always listen to your dreams and be supportive.)*

_____

_____

_____

6. *Your goals. (What great thing, or things, did you want to accomplish in your lifetime? Did you want to be a figure skater or a tennis champ or the first woman astronaut or president of the United States? Or were your dreams about more realistic goals, like being a good mom or wife?)*

_____

_____

_____

7. *Life in general. Now write a paragraph describing, in general, what you expected life to be like. You may use several of the dreams you listed above in your description. Remember, the more information you give about your dreams, the more useful it will be in determining where those dreams come from.*

_____

_____

_____

Once you have completed this reflection, you may real-ize, as Jan did, that many (or most) of your dreams remain unfulfilled. Some, you might agree, will never be realized; they will remain fantasies—just fun things to think about once in a while. Others may stir up feelings of pain or re-gret. Perhaps some of these dreams were on their way to being realized at one time but were crushed by choices made by others, or by unavoidable painful circumstances that came unexpectedly into your life. Yet each dream tells a part of the story about who you are and will give you valu-able clues to patterns in your life that need to be understood and resolved.

In the next chapter, we will look at how these dreams are shaped by our unmet needs, some of which begin in child-hood, so we can understand why our dreams have such a strong influence on our lives today.

—5—

Dreams: The Story of Our Unmet Needs

Mary was a woman many women envy—she had lovely white skin, high cheek-bones, raven black hair, a beautiful figure, and the money to buy the most stylish clothes, made of expensive, elegant fabrics. On the surface, everything about Mary's childhood seemed to be just as ideal; she had been raised in a lovely suburb by parents who were known for their kindness and community and church service. Yet she felt that something was missing.

"I was really lonely growing up, and many times fanta-sized that my 'real parents' would come and rescue me, even though I knew I wasn't adopted," she told us.

When we asked her to describe what she wanted to be rescued from, she couldn't point to "anything that awful—just this ongoing feeling of loneliness."

"What would have changed in your life if your 'real par-ents' had come?" we asked, still searching for a clue to her unhappiness. Mary thought a while and then described her childhood dream. "I always imagined my 'real parents' as warm, exciting people. They would whisk me off to some new place, filled with fun people and activities. I guess we never did anything fun in my family. I can only remember going on a vacation one time."

"What about those dreams? Describe them for us."

"I often dreamed we would live in another country, like France or Switzerland. I would have a warm, open, and caring husband, who not only was involved with me, but was involved with our children as well. We would travel a lot, always meeting people who were fascinating and knowledgeable. I guess that almost sounds like a *Sound of Music* ending—at least the family part."

Mary was telling us a great deal about herself and her childhood needs as she described those dreams to us. Often our dreams are the result of our unfilled needs.

ADULT DREAMS BUILD ON UNMET CHILDHOOD NEEDS

Our dreams usually begin as a response to some need that was overlooked, neglected, or unfulfilled in our childhood. That need was (and still is) met through the dream. Therefore, our dreams give us important information about the wounded parts within ourselves. And when our dreams are frustrated, we not only feel disappointment but we suffer additional harm to that injured part of us.

Mary's two dreams give some important information about her childhood. Even though her family life was fine on the surface, Mary felt a deep emotional emptiness. A parent doesn't have to be overtly abusive for a child to dream that "someday my real parents will come." An emotionally absent parent may cause the child to feel the same way.

Mary's adult expectations about her life were built on the dreams she had in childhood, and those dreams were built on the unmet needs she experienced as a child. The illustration below shows the beginning of our cycle of disappointment. (We will follow this cycle throughout the book to its final completion—either depression and despair or hope and fulfillment.)

This cycle is like a heavy chain, which begins as an individual link—our unmet needs—and becomes heavier as each consecutive link is added. Finally, the weight becomes overbearing, and we are bound by depression.

Unmet   Childhood   Adult

•——— shape ———•——— shape ———•

Needs   Dreams   Expectations

The Chain of Disappointment

Put Mary in that equation, for instance. *Her unmet need* for warmth and affection from her parents shaped *her childhood dreams* of the "real parents" who would rescue her, which shaped *her adult expectation* to live in a chalet in Switzerland and meet people who were exciting (who probably wore lederhosen or long cotton skirts with embroidered suspenders and blouses, like the von Trapp family).

Now put yourself in that equation: "My unmet need for _____ shaped my childhood dream of _____, which in turn shaped my adult expectation _____."

In our counseling we have found that our early unmet needs usually are connected to our basic need to feel connected and/or our basic need to be autonomous. Both needs are critical to the development of a healthy individual.

1. Our Need to Be Connected ("Mommy and I are one.")

All of us need to be emotionally connected to a nurturing, loving person. That connection was perfect within our mother's womb; there we were safe and warm and fed in a blissful state of oneness. As newborns, we left the paradise where every need was satisfied before we even experienced it and entered a cold, bright, harsh environment that felt totally unsafe. (There's that setup again.) The world forced its reality upon us, thrusting us away from the safe union with our mother and leaving us to fend for ourselves.

In her book *Necessary Losses,* Judith Viorst wrote about this connection between the infant and the mother: "Although we do not remember it, we also never forget it. We acknowledge a paradise and a paradise lost. We acknowledge a time of harmony, wholeness, unbreachable safety, unconditional love, and a time when that wholeness was irretrievably rent."[1]

Again and again we experience the powerful need for the safety of that union—the need to reconnect to our mother. Children who for various reasons cannot connect with their mother desperately long for that connection, a feeling similar to the pain an adult feels at the death of a loved one.

At the end of World War II, many children who were lying alone in cribs in orphanages in England were dying from marasmus, a wasting away of the body, even though they were being properly fed and cared for. Researchers set out to determine why. Surprisingly, one orphanage in the war-torn areas did not have a high death rate; instead, its rate was the same as the general population's. The researchers could find only one difference between this orphanage and the others: a nurse named Anna, who took it upon herself to hold each of the children as she went about her work. That brief connection with another human being meant the difference between life and death for babies who had been separated from their parents. The results of that study confirmed an infant's deep need to feel attached to a caring mother.

Human touch is essential, as this study proves, but we

also long for much more—we want love, warmth, and a feeling of connection, as Mary did. Yet, once we leave the womb, our mother has to choose to meet our needs, so she doesn't always do as good a job. She acts imperfectly, out of her own neediness, simply because she is human. In addition, some of our needs as infants conflicted with one another—we wanted two opposing things at the same time—so they couldn't both be met.

Since it is not possible for any human to go through the early years of childhood perfectly connected, the ideal mother has been lovingly called the "good-enough mother" by Margaret Mahler, child psychologist and the author of *The Psychological Birth of the Human Infant.*

Unfortunately, some of us did not have a "good-enough" mother. Our mother may have had fears and doubts about her ability to take care of us, and we experienced those feelings from her, making our need for emotional connectedness and safety even stronger.

The cycle goes like this: Mom has her own deficits, her own unmet needs, which she then transfers to her infant. The infant feels the mother's anxiety or fear, needs her even more, and thus, becomes more demanding. The more demanding the infant becomes, the more anxiety or fear the mother experiences. Because the emotionally damaged infant is not able to give love back to the mother, the unmet needs of both the mother and her child continue feeding off each other and are multiplied exponentially. As the cycle spins on and on, the infant begins to suffer emotional damage from unsafe feelings of anxiety and fear.

Sometimes Dad can fill in for Mom, but he may be absent or so emotionally stretched out due to the ongoing pressures of his job that he doesn't have much emotional support to give baby either. Or Mom and Dad may already have five children, as Mary's family did, and may be too busy to give the new addition to the family as much love as they have given the other children.

One woman was damaged by her mother's adherence to an old theory of child rearing: schedule feeding. The woman's mother had been told by her mother and her pediatrician, "The baby must be fed on a schedule, every four hours during the day. No sooner, no later."

When this woman had her first child, she did what her mother had done to her. "I used to turn up the radio so I wouldn't hear the baby crying, it hurt me so," the woman told us.

Imagine how this baby felt. Her needs were being met on a schedule, not when she felt hungry so obviously she did not feel her mother's care and affection. Instead, she felt as lonely and estranged from her mother as Mary did. (This mom thought for herself the next time around and raised her other two children on a demand feeding schedule, but that couldn't remedy the emotional distance between her and her firstborn daughter.)

If we add to these deficits the traumatically painful experiences of a child who is abandoned or abused or otherwise hurt by the loss of a parent, the child is going to be even more frustrated, more needy, more disappointed.

When we experience a lack of emotional connectedness early in our lives, we grow up with a fear that if we really care about someone, they will abandon us. Our dreams will often include the idea of someone—usually a husband—who will come into our lives and make us feel secure. These unmet needs for emotional connection lay the foundation for many of our expectations in our marriage and other relationships.

Mary's dream of living someplace that sounded exotic was an attempt to resolve her loneliness. "People over there" would be far more interesting than "people here," and they would be easier to meet. What she didn't say (probably because she was unaware of it) was, "It is always easier to control the closeness we experience with people over there." You can keep your distance from people who are "far away." And, of course, she felt safe because those people only existed in her dream.

Several patterns can emerge out of this neediness, like Mary's difficulty in experiencing closeness with another person. Her inner fear of being abandoned, and her fear of the pain that would result, made it difficult for her to ever trust anyone. Yet she did not see this fear as the cause of her lack of intimacy with her husband or her friends. Instead, she blamed a personality trait—aggressiveness—in the other person that made her feel "unsafe." Mary became so "picky" about her friends, she eventually discouraged most of them.

We have also seen patients who had the opposite problem—they connected too quickly with someone else because of their neediness and their fear of abandonment. This inability to maintain a comfortable distance in their relationship often contributes to the other person pulling away from them and eventually doing what they fear the most—abandoning them. (We will talk more about how our unmet childhood needs trigger our adult behavior in the next chapter.)

Believe it or not, even if our mother meets our every need, she can set us up for a whole different set of problems. If we have a mother who meets most of our needs, we may never learn to delay gratification and to deal with pain and loss. Instead, we may feel an unhealthy sense of entitlement.

A False Sense of Entitlement   We all feel entitled to happiness at some time. "I deserve to have a house as nice as my neighbors or a husband as kind or kids who are as outstanding." Entitlement is the idea, "Life owes me," and it usually has its roots in the early stages of our lives. (The women we mentioned earlier who experienced a lack of emotional connectedness with their mothers can also have a sense of "being owed.")

Sometimes children with special needs or those who are very ill and come near death are treated differently by their parents. These children are so protected that almost every wish of theirs is quickly fulfilled. Of course, parents who play favorites with a particular child or spoil their children also give their children an unhealthy sense of entitlement.

These children do not understand what is going on; they simply enjoy the benefits of their position and come to expect it. Yet when they are adults, other people do not treat them as special as Mom or Dad did.

Two things usually happen when our dreams are fueled by this sense of entitlement. First, the sense of "being owed" keeps us focused on what we do not have. We feel "The world owes me something," even though we can't say exactly what or why. Second, our frustration level for the realities of life is usually very low, so when we encounter difficulties, we give up our dreams more quickly.

As a child, Becky had a mysterious, life-threatening disease. The doctors were never able to identify it, so she almost died several times. She was only two at the time and has no memory of that traumatic period. But her older siblings do remember, and they say their mother abandoned the family during and after Becky's illness, devoting every waking minute to her.

As Becky described her dreams to us, she realized she always placed herself in a special position. She was going to marry a wealthy man who would always take care of her. Along with her status as his wife, there would be a lot of public recognition for all the contributions she and her husband made to society. Becky never even thought about a career. She only imagined all the great things she and her husband would do for others.

Becky actually did marry a wealthy man, and she and her husband were involved in a lot of charitable activities. But if Becky wasn't the focus of attention, she moved on to something else. She was struggling with a feeling of entitlement.

Even though Becky got her chance to live out her dream through her husband's wealth, she was disappointed by the superficiality of her relationships. "I felt as if no one really accepted me just because I am me." She was in a bind— wanting to be accepted for herself and also wanting to be put on a pedestal. Underlying that was the fact that she couldn't accept herself for who she was. Her alienation from everyone, including herself, only deepened her incredible loneliness. Eventually, her disappointment led to a serious depression, the result of most long-term disappointments.

Someone once said life deals harshly with us in two ways: One is to be denied our dreams, the other is to be granted our dreams. Only recently was Becky able to see that the special way her mother had treated her as she was growing up had distanced her from her brother and sister, as well as from her father. As a result, she never really knew how to relate to anyone, except by somehow being special.

Our first need, as infants, is for a oneness with another person, which almost feels like the warmth and safety of the womb. From birth to eight months, the baby needs to be connected to the mother. Then, we begin to become aware of another need—the need to be autonomous, a need that also causes us to dream our dreams.

2. Our Need to Be Autonomous ("I Want to Be Me!")

Balancing our need for emotional connectedness to some significant person is our need to be independent. We have to learn to say "No" in life as well as "Yes." When we say "No," we begin to develop our own sense of individuality and separateness from our mother and father. (Parents sometimes see this as "the terrible twos." Instead, it's a healthy step toward maturity.)

The beginning of this separation experience is called "hatching" by Mahler and others. Obviously, it is more than just saying "No." It basically involves a shift from being inner-directed (when a child explores his or her own body) to being outward-directed (when a child begins to explore the external world). This shift is accelerated as a child begins to stand, and then eventually walk on his or her own.

After a child makes her first move towards separation, there should be a time when she moves back towards her mother. But there is a difference. A taste of your own sense of self keeps you from moving back into the earlier symbiotic fusion with your mother. To do that would negate your steps towards autonomy. In healthy development, this "coming back to the mother" is called "rapprochement," a bringing together again. (Mothers recognize this as marking the end of the "terrible twos.")

Connection comes first. Then, within the safety of that close relationship, the child can effectively move toward being a separate, autonomous person. These two needs seem to be contradictory, but they are actually complimentary. They run side by side on parallel tracks, as this diagram of an infant's development shows:

Birth	**6–8 months**	**15–18 months**	**3–4 years**

The Need to Be Connected
(Learning How to Trust)

Eventually We Integrate

The Need to Be Autonomous
(Learning How to Be Independent)

A Child's Development   If we hit the terrible twos and haven't made the connection with Mom, we won't have the safety to begin to assert our will and "act like a typical two year old." Either we won't feel secure enough in our emotional connection with Mom, or we can't say "No" to her because she is such an overpowering presence. In either case, the anxiety of being separate from mother is simply too frightening because we fear the loss of mother.

All of us experience this fear of losing Mother when she goes away (that's why kids cry when they see the babysitter), but the safety of a good emotional connection with Mother allows us to move beyond that fear towards autonomy. If our emotional connection is tenuous, however, our adult relationships take on the characteristic of being too smothering or too controlling. One reason we may react this way is because the new person may appear to threaten our relationship with one or both parents. We operate under the belief that our moves away from Mom and Dad and toward another person will hurt or even destroy our parents.

Sometimes the opposite occurs, and we are pushed towards separateness by a mother who is too busy or who is uncomfortable with our neediness as an infant. These circumstances force us to develop a sense of independence long before we are ready for autonomy. Later on, we may value this sense of independence, overlooking the loss of connectedness as the price we pay.

Some women in our survey were raised to believe that staying at home is good and moving away is bad. Often their first steps towards autonomy went unsupported, so they took those steps completely on their own. As a result, they dreamed of being more independent in adulthood but avoided it because they had been led to believe it was wrong. They made do, rather than going after something that is so important. These women's adult dreams often had a theme of escape, like Mary's, so they could be empowered to control the degree of closeness they experienced in them. Here again, their unmet need to be autonomous formed the theme for their dreams.

Other women's dreams included the ideas of space and openness; they seemed to be responding to the intrusiveness of a parent who limited their space. But autonomy is more than space or geography, as these women found out. Some of them moved across the country in an effort to separate themselves from a parent, only to discover that once they got there, nothing had changed. The emotional distance remained the same; they still felt crowded and controlled.

Our unmet needs shape our dreams. So do parental expectations, experiences later in life, cultural influences, and our beliefs about life.

OTHER FACTORS THAT SHAPE OUR DREAMS

Parental Expectations Shape Our Dreams

Sometimes our dreams are built around either our response to our parents' excessive expectations of us or the opposite, their lack of expectations for us. Cheri Fuller says in her book, *Motivating Your Kids from Crayons to Career,* "Sometimes children are limited by their parents' low expectations." And "Sometimes parents' expectations are so high, a child feels he can never measure up."[2]

Sometimes we want to prove that a parent's ideas about us are wrong; we can do more than he or she thought we could. One woman said, "My dream of completing my college education was a reaction against my father's belief that I was not capable of obtaining a college degree." She eventually finished, after starting and stopping a number of times over a period of years. Her desire for her father's approval helped form a dream that drove her to finish, regardless of her age or the obstacles that presented themselves over the years.

Another woman had the opposite experience. "My determination to finish college, going part-time for almost twelve years, was the result of my father's saying to me over and over again, 'Make sure you prepare yourself for life by getting a college degree. Don't be like me.'" His belief that she could accomplish that goal helped her persevere until she finally finished.

Parental expectations, whether positive or negative, have a powerful effect on us. Both women built their dreams around their fathers' expectations—one in reaction against it, the other in response to it. The child who follows in a parent's footsteps and the child who carefully avoids anything the parent does, even though talented in that area, are responding to the same dynamic.

Experiences in Adolescence Shape Our Dreams

Currently, many psychologists are focusing on childhood trauma, but not all emotional trauma that shapes our adult dreams occurs in early childhood. The National Association for Mental Health lists a child's eight basic emotional needs in its publication "What Every Child Needs for Good Mental Health": love, acceptance, security, protection, independence, faith, guidance, and control. These needs can lead to death if unmet.[3] The adolescent's struggle for love and acceptance is an example. But there are crises in adolescence as well.

Katie talked about how difficult adolescence was for her. Prior to puberty, she had felt comfortable in her family and was fairly popular with her peer group at school. At puberty, the changes in her physical appearance added six inches to her height and no additional weight to her body.

"I felt ugly," she said, "I was all too aware of my gangly, awkward, skinny shape and started to withdraw from most of my friends."

Katie tried to talk about her feelings with her mom, but her mom brushed aside her concerns. "It will all work out," she said. "You will fill out soon enough."

On the other hand Dad almost seemed disappointed in her appearance. Instead of roughhousing with her, as he did before, he now seemed distant. He was willing to talk about school and her studies, but never affirmed her as a pretty, feminine woman. "I could sense an awkwardness in him as a response to my own awkwardness," she said.

Katie started spending a lot of time on her studies and became an avid reader. As she read novels, she dreamed. "In my dream, I looked different. I was a graceful, beautiful, fully developed woman. Instead of ignoring me, men wanted to be with me. My dream even included my father telling me he was sorry."

Katie is now in her mid-thirties, and even though everyone who knows her would agree she has become a beautiful woman, she still feels like the awkward junior-high student whenever she is around other people, especially men her own age. She sees her dad as a distant, judging authority figure, even though her mother insists he doesn't feel that way.

"I've been more successful in my work than I ever imagined I would," Katie continued. "God has really blessed my career. Why can't He bless my relationships?" Katie's dreams are still shaped by that awkward girl inside.

Cultural Influences Shape Our Dreams

If you live in the United States, you live in the country of the American Dream: Even the little guy can make it big— here in America. Actress Linda Evans said, "This is a land where we can dare to dream and make our dreams come true." Newspaper columnist Ann Landers commented, "No matter what color you are or what background you come from, you can make it big if you work hard enough." Beverly Sills, the well loved opera singer, said, "I'm a walking example of the American Dream. I never thought my dream of becoming an opera singer was an impossibility." And Estée Lauder, founder of the popular line of cosmetics, pointed out the sexual equality of the American dream, "Women in most other countries aren't allowed to build financial empires."[4]

In fact, recent political campaigns have focused on keeping the American dream alive for our children so they can have the same wonderful opportunities. Even though we all hope that this dream will come true for us, most of us will never achieve the spectacular personal or financial success the dream promises.

We are also influenced by other cultural dreams, which are reinforced by television and print advertising. Many people define the ideal family as television's Cleaver family of "Leave it to Beaver" or the Huxtables of "The Cosby Show." As children we watch these shows and expect our families to be like them or we may see a movie shot in an exotic part of the world, and dream that we will travel there someday. We watch a television documentary about someone's success in business, and we dream that we can do the same thing when we grow up.

For years, many of us have felt we could resist the effects of our culture, not only on our dreams and expectations, but also on the pace of life we live. More and more, as time passes, we are impressed with how powerful these cultural forces really are, and how much they shape our lives, even when we are actively resisting them.

Our need to be connected and our need for autonomy,

our parental expectations, our experiences in adolescence and later in life, our cultural influences, and finally our beliefs about life shape our dreams.

Our Beliefs about Life Shape Our Dreams

If we hold the viewpoint that "Life is meant to be fair" or "Right will always win in the end," those beliefs will shape and color our dreams and intensify our disappointments.

Anne grew up in a family with strong religious beliefs, and those beliefs became an important part of her own life. When she went off to college, she felt she could be content either single or married, as long as she knew it was a part of God's plan for her.

While attending college, she met the man who would later become her husband. "We did everything the right way. We took our time with the relationship, not wanting to rush things and make a mistake. Neither of us felt like we had to get married. We dated casually for over a year, and were more like good friends than boyfriend and girlfriend. As our relationship became more serious, we talked about our relationship with faculty members we both respected. We went through a premarital counseling course with our church, and then even went to a professional counselor for counsel and advice about how to make the adjustments we both knew would be part of life together.

"Our families were important to both of us, so we talked with our parents, and even our grandparents. Everyone thought we made a great couple. Some of our friends said we were being too cautious, but I think they admired our preparation and care."

All through their courtship Anne and her fiancé struggled to keep the sexual part of their relationship under control. Both of them were virgins when they got married. In Anne's words, "We did everything right!"

"But then," Anne added, "things started to change as the wedding day grew closer. I saw glimpses of a different side of my husband-to-be. I passed off those observations as just a normal part of premarital nervousness and the stress of the wedding, but he started to verbally attack me on our wedding night, and he hasn't stopped since. He's abusive: there's no other word for it. He's a crazy-maker. But when I'm in tears, he's suddenly repentant, promising never to do it again. But he never keeps his promises. I don't even listen to his apologies anymore—they mean nothing!"

When Anne shared her disappointment in her marriage with her mother, her parents said they had never really agreed with Anne's marriage. "They said they only went along with it because they felt their opinion didn't matter anyway. I felt totally betrayed," Anne said. "Why didn't they tell me the truth? And if God loves me and wants to protect me, why would He let me marry a man who is so painful to live with? I gave God every opportunity to stop me. My hopes were dashed by my husband, but I think my greatest disappointment is with God."

Anne's disappointment in her marriage was intensified by her belief that "Right will always win in the end." If someone does everything right, she will be rewarded accordingly.

Another woman, Shirley, told us how she struggled with her disappointment when her daughter announced that she was pregnant and broke off their relationship. Shirley struggled with the idea of fairness—she had done the best she knew how as a mother; it wasn't fair for her daughter to treat her so badly. Although she agreed that life wasn't always fair, she said, "I never thought it would be like this!" Her belief that "Life is meant to be fair" added to the intensity and depth of her disappointment.

We've looked at some of the sources of our dreams. Understanding what has shaped our expectations tells us what has been missing in our lives. If we identify the unmet needs at work within our dreams, we can understand our wounded parts. These wounds are behind the patterns of behavior that get us into trouble.

Personal Reflections:
Your Unmet Needs

Think again about the dreams you described in Chapter 4. What themes can you find in these dreams?

Jan's chart looked like this:

My Dream	Theme
1. Be a professional ice skater and tennis player	Performing the best
2. Owning that big house with pillars	Having people admire me, being special, unique
3. Having everyone around me	Having people like me
4. To be a super-mom and an artist	Accomplishing a lot; Being the center of my kids' lives

Now list three of your dreams that influenced the expectations you have today:

My Dream	Theme
_____	_____
_____	_____
_____	_____

Can you identify a repeated theme in these dreams?

Each of Jan's dreams, for instance, places her in a position of feeling special and unique. Another repeated theme is her desire to be loved and accepted. As the youngest of five children, Jan struggled to feel special and worked hard at separating herself so she could "stand out in the crowd."

You might come up with a couple of common themes in your own dreams:

_____

_____

_____

_____

Since many of Jan's dreams revolved around the theme of being special and wanting to be loved, she can begin to identify what strongly motivates her. These themes are related to her unmet childhood needs, and perhaps other unfulfilled needs in her life.

Now think of the need your dream is trying to fulfill. (We are looking for clues that tell us what motivates us right now.)
Check the ones that apply to you.

Indicators of the basic need for connectedness:

_____ Need to be loved

_____ Need for acceptance

_____ Need for guidance

_____ Need for security and need for protection

Indicators of the basic need for autonomy:

____ *Need for independence*

____ *Need for faith*

____ *Need for control*

Now list your themes below and the need the dream is trying to fulfill. Finally use the third column to record if that need falls under the basic need of being connected or being autonomous.

For example, Jan's theme of needing to feel special points to the area of connectedness. Her chart would look like this:

My Themes	My Need	Being Connected or Autonomous
1. Feeling special	To feel loved	To be connected
2. Lots of people	To feel accepted	To be connected

"My basic need was to be special to my mom, who was probably tired and may not have had a whole lot of emotional closeness to give her fifth child," Jan says. "Even though I had lots of attention from my siblings, that did not completely fill the void. I needed to be connected with Mom. So I probably had deficits in the area of connectedness, and my dreams made up for that unmet basic need."

My Themes	My Need	Being Connected or Autonomous
____	____	____
____	____	____
____	____	____

All our unmet childhood needs feed into our adult behavior, affecting the decisions we make everyday and causing us to add other links to the chain of disappointment. Eventually our disappointment will lead to depression. We'll look at how that happens in Part Two, "From Disappointment to Depression." And we will begin with our adult behaviors and how they are influenced by the childhood needs we just identified.

— PART II —

From Disappointment to Depression

—6—

How Could It All Go So Wrong?

T he winter sun was pouring warmly through the tall windows in our dining room, making the candles Jan had placed on the table soft to the touch. How pretty it all looked, with the colorfully painted wooden crèche figures and the glass ornaments spread out in the sun. Dave and Jan had unpacked the Christmas tapes first and put on the familiar music to a slightly higher volume than they usually tolerated. After all it was early in the season, only the day after Thanksgiving, and they were determined to get the holiday off to a great start.

The decorations were piled high on the table as Dave unpacked each box.

"Don't put any more things up here until I've had a chance to organize the stuff!" Jan admonished.

"Okay," Dave responded, with a cheerful cooperation that took her by surprise. When it came to doing work together Jan knew she was bossy; she was trying to work on it, but she knew that she had been pushing it all day as she directed this operation.

Jan's expectations were running extremely high. This Christmas was going to be one of the best ever. She could just feel it. All their family—Greg and his new wife and even Dave's mom and dad—would be together for the first time in many years. Many Christmas holidays had not been so good for them, and as Jan looked through the decorations she caught herself briefly reaching back into the past, capturing the feelings of those painful Christmastimes, seeing them as vividly and as accurately as if they had happened yesterday. *Those are past,* she told herself as she shook off the shadow that began to press in upon the beautiful day.

Jan had been busy all Thanksgiving week, making her usual endless lists of things to accomplish and, of course, making another list of all the things she intended to ask Dave to do.

"Let me look at your list," Dave would ask as he saw her sitting at the table in the evening. He knew better, though. Jan never let him look at her lists because she knew that he would question each item, wondering in a protective sort of way if she really had to do this or that.

So Jan kept her lists to herself. Her theory was, "If I thought it was important enough to be on my list, then it will stay there until it is time to cross it off." The lists for this Christmas were long, and Jan knew Dave would be appalled at the things she wanted to do.

Together they dragged the ladder into the living room and began the task of decorating. Jan liked to decorate everywhere. This meant that they took the usual pictures down from the walls and replaced them with Christmas pictures or greenery and wreaths; they draped everything that stood and some things that they created especially for the season. And they decorated the bathrooms and the bedrooms.

"All so unnecessary," Dave had said at one time. "Who's going to see it there?" he had ventured to ask.

"We are, of course." It seemed so perfectly reasonable to Jan. By December twenty-fourth, Jan was exhausted. The family had arrived two weeks before, and cooking big meals had absolutely worn her out. But both Dave and she were still in a somewhat cheerful mood. Jan was delighted to have everyone around, people talking in the kitchen, hovering around the food, helping, grandchildren making messes; that's her style (and her dream, remember).

Retreating to read a magazine or straining to hear the sound of the television over the din of voices is more Dave's style. But both Jan and Dave were surprisingly accepting of what each needed for this special holiday.

Christmas Eve is always the highlight of the Stoop family Christmas, even though no one opens any gifts until Christmas morning. On Christmas Eve they share special verbal gifts with each other (like appreciating someone's patience or courage to face a task), and then take Communion. Each year they try to blend the same traditional activities with a new, creative way to introduce the sharing time. Dave was in charge of it this year.

That is, he was supposed to be in charge of it. This Christmas he and Jan had talked about it early. Dave said, "Worry no more about it—take it off your list—I've got it under control."

To Jan those were alarming words. To a person like Jan who must oversee everything and who struggles to remain in control of almost everything, it is a bit scary to hear someone say, "Don't worry about it." Nevertheless, Jan decided to hand over the responsibility to Dave.

"I had so much else to think about with planning the dinner and setting the table. And besides, I had come down with a terrible cold that morning, the kind that just drips no matter what you take to stop it.

"It's going well, I thought to myself as we all piled into the car to go to the Christmas Eve service. Except for a few minor hangups like a lost pacifier, we made it to the church and then back to the house to have dinner."

By then Dave and Eric had decided that they were going to finish dinner, as Mom shouldn't be near the food with a cold. *Fine with me,* Jan thought.

The dinner went off without a hitch, with Eric serving it beautifully and Dave making the last-minute preparations. The dishes were cleared, dessert was finished, and the family sat there for what seemed to be an eternity. Of course, Jan was wondering when Dave would introduce the verbal gift sharing. She waited and waited—at least that's what she thought she did.

Jan could feel the warmth rising in her face as she tried to quell her feelings of deep disappointment—Dave was not going to do as he said. Then Jan decided, *Someone has to say something.* So she took over. She suggested how they might each share. As she did, she could see by the look on Dave's face that she had done the wrong thing.

Jan paused and looked straight at Dave. "Did you have something you wanted to say?"

"Nope," Dave answered.

Even though Jan got cold looks from Dave, she avoided his glare and pressed right on. They somehow got through the evening without causing too much disturbance to the other family members, but they both knew that there were presents yet to wrap, and things to be said, which would not be said that night. They fell asleep that Christmas Eve not speaking to each other.

Christmas morning was delightful. Their children and grandchildren, along with the great-grandparents, were all awakened early by Colleen's shouts of delight. Yet they couldn't complain; she had slept through the night, even without the pacifier. But Dave and Jan had not slept well at all.

Later Christmas night, with everyone quietly in bed, Jan and Dave tried to sort it all out with each other. "How come you are the one acting so angry?" Jan asked.

"What do you mean, 'How come I'm the one?'" Dave said.

"I mean I'm the one who is disappointed. I trusted you! You said you would take care of it," Jan retorted as the stinging tears began to flow.

"Take care of it? You jumped right in and took over before I even had half a chance. I had this thing all planned, and I had really worked hard on it, and you just took it away from me. Just like that!"

"You're angry! How can you be so angry? I asked you to do something, you didn't do it, and so I feel so disappointed. I knew that I had to do something. How long did you want me to wait? An hour or two? You do this all the time!"

Over the next several days, each time they tried to talk about what happened that evening, Jan insisted that her disappointment was devastating; she had trusted him, and he had let her down. The more she insisted, the more he insisted he had the right to be angry. And the more deeply Jan felt her disappointment.

Even though the Christmas incident took place months before this book was written, Jan could still remember her feelings of disappointment as she wrote about this incident. We hang on to our dreams, and her disappointment had a history of other disappointments (old feelings of being let down as a child, just as Dave had let her down) and a history of dreams (all those expectations of what her own family would be like, especially during the holidays: "Decorations, food, and meaningful traditions would abound."). And those dreams influenced her quick action to fill in for Dave.

UNMET CHILDHOOD NEEDS FEED
INTO ADULT BEHAVIORS

Sarah grew up in what many call "a traditional family," where the mother stays home to raise her children. "Dad wasn't around very much," she told us, "but he was very responsible, many times working two jobs so we could live comfortably, but frugally, without my mom having to work. In many ways, our family seemed ideal."

When we asked Sarah about some of the dreams she had as a child, she said, "I often thought about what it would be like when my brother and sister and I grew up and had our own kids—how we would enjoy being together with our families. I guess I was longing for some emotional connection with my family as a child, but I didn't understand that I couldn't really make it happen, so I escaped into a dream where I could experience it in the future."

She had put her father on a pedestal, as a hard-working dad who acted very responsibly for his family, but she now realized the many ways in which he had abandoned his family for his work.

Sarah went on to describe what happened when she left home and got married. "I had absolutely no emotional closeness with my first husband. We married young, and I think he just wanted someone to take care of him as his mother had. During the twelve years we were married, he was totally preoccupied with his work. We divorced after he left me for another woman. I've been married to my present husband for thirteen years, and there is no emotional closeness in this marriage either." Her unmet childhood need for closeness (to be connected) continually affected her relationship with her husband.

Sarah discovered just how unloving her family was when her mother had a stroke and her parents came to live with her for six months. Her brother and sister offered to help out, but they seldom came over to Sarah's house to see their parents, let alone do anything to help.

"When my mother was living in my home," Sarah continued, "I saw her as physically weak and emotionally needy for the first time in my life. She reached out and asked for support from my father for the first time in her life, yet he never gave it. That made me face the emptiness of their relationship. I've come to realize, with the help of a therapist, that even though I may have traveled a lot of miles over the years, emotionally I am still in the same place."

Sarah's experience has added another link to the chain of disappointment:

Unmet	Childhood	Adult	Adult
•— shape —•	— shape —•	— shape —•	
Needs	Dreams	Expectations	Behaviors

That chain played out in Sarah's life as follows: Her *unmet needs* (her desire for connectedness) shaped her *childhood dreams* (of her sister and brother and their families being close as adults), which shaped her *adult expectations* (a close relationship with her husband and a closely knit family of her own), which shaped her *adult behaviors* (her distant relationship with her two husbands because she never had a close, loving relationship with her dad).

The disappointing relationship between Sarah and her husband was almost identical to what her mother had experienced in her marriage with her father, and it resulted in the same emptiness Sarah had experienced with her father. Sarah was unaware of this destructive chain until we helped her recognize these unmet needs buried in her childhood.

Now think again about your own unmet needs and fill in the chain from your own life. "My unmet need for _____ shaped my childhood dream of _____, which in turn shaped my adult expectation

of _____, which shaped my adult behavior of
_____."

Sarah's experience illustrates what happens to many of us as we attempt to fulfill our childhood dreams in our adult lives; we get caught in a cycle of contradictory beliefs, which in turn influences our behavior.

THE BACK AND FORTH OF CONTRADICTORY BELIEFS

Once we have failed to fulfill our childhood dreams and begin to experience disappointment, we are faced with two seemingly contradictory beliefs. We believe someone else is to blame for our disappointment at the same time that we blame ourselves for our disappointments.

I. We believe someone else is to blame for our disappointment.

Since many of our early hurts and disappointments were caused by someone else, we think we can protect ourselves against further disappointment by finding someone who will do just the opposite of what these hurtful people did to us in the past. We deduct, "Since the problem is someone else, the solution will also be someone else." In Sarah's case, she believed that the right "Mr. Someone" was going to come into her life and make all of her dreams come true.

We look to parents, friends, husbands, mother institutions (schools, government agencies, and the church), things, work, money, and children to solve our problems. Our focus is on anyone or anything that can be blamed for our disappointments.

At the same time we also blame ourselves.

2. We believe we are to blame for our disappointment.

Sarah developed the belief that she was solely responsible for making certain her dreams became a reality. "If I depend on anyone else, I'll just be disappointed again," she reasoned. When "Mr. Someone," her first husband, didn't perform as expected, she began working to fulfill her dreams by shaping up "Mr. Someone."

Sarah began fluctuating back and forth between these two contradictory beliefs, just as we all do. Once she realized she couldn't make "Mr. Someone" into her dream man, she moved back to her first belief. "Mr. Someone" was not "Mr. Right." So now she began again to find "Mr. Right," the man who would make her dreams come true. The answer is still someone else, but it's someone who, this time, really will fulfill our dreams. Like Sarah, some of us tenaciously hold on to belief Number One—that someone else will "fix the problems" and make our dreams come true.

Others may stay stuck with belief Number Two—it is our fault that our dreams are unfulfilled. We embark on a never-ending journey to fix ourselves and everyone around us. This cycle of contradictory beliefs directly influences our behavior.

Now new links are added to the chain of disappointment, spinning us deeper and deeper into our pain. The chain has grown even longer and looks something like the chart on page 98.

No matter which belief we become stuck in, we are thrust back into our dream in order to avoid the pain of disappointment. However, each time we hold on to our dream, we set ourselves up for additional hurt and loss, and we start living our lives from one disappointment to another.

SIMPLE OR COMPLEX DISAPPOINTMENTS

Some disappointments are so devastating that they threaten to destroy us, while others are easily managed and forgotten. Some are what we call simple disappointments

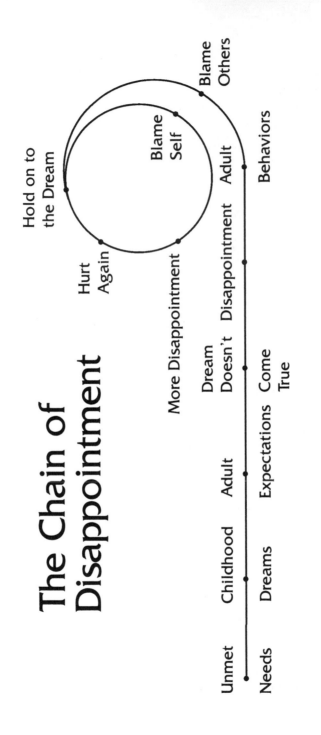

and others are complex disappointments. Let's look at each.

Simple Disappointments

Not all disappointments are as painful or devastating as Sarah's. Some disappointments we experience, even though unpleasant and painful, have little lasting impact on our lives. For example, when the person who cuts our hair botches the job, our disappointment may be acute, but we know our hair will grow back.

Simple disappointments are best defined as "single-episode disappointments." A special dinner we have been looking forward to is postponed or a trip we were anticipating is canceled or a word of appreciation from our boss is never received—these episodes fit into the category of simple disappointments.

These simple disappointments affect us differently depending on how much time or energy we have invested in the outcome. We may have looked forward to that special dinner for several weeks, to the thank you from our boss for several hours, or to the promised trip for several months, but because they involve relatively short periods of time, we can usually get over these disappointments fairly quickly.

However, that doesn't mean that simple disappointments don't affect us. Many simple disappointments can hurt deeply, such as the breakup of a relationship or the end of a job or the failure to get a hoped-for promotion. The loss of Jan's velvet snowsuit caused her profound pain as a child even though, taken alone, it would be considered a simple disappointment. Recovery from such deeper simple disappointments may take longer, but they are still defined as simple because they are single episodes. They are not part of a pattern of behavior.

It is easy to learn from our simple disappointments, especially when they hurt us deeply. Since they are single-episode events, they have a "startle" effect on us; we notice them right away. They are not allowed to become part of a pattern.

Smaller disappointments, however, can add to the internal reservoir of hurts and disappointments we have accumulated over the years. That's when a seemingly small disappointment can push us beyond our limit. It's just one more, but it's one too many.

If we have earlier or later experiences of losing something important which are added to the loss of that "velvet snowsuit," the simple disappointment becomes a complex disappointment.

Complex Disappointments

The front of our brochure for the Minirth-Meier West inpatient treatment program reads: "If the disappointments and problems of life came one at a time, most anyone could deal with them. Unfortunately that seldom happens. . . ."

Disappointments come right on top of one another. They pile up and overlap until we have a hard time distinguishing one from the other. Long after the disappointing event is over, the deep feelings of disappointment linger— sometimes for days, sometimes for months, and sometimes for years. When one disappointment connects to another, the cumulative effect is so powerful and causes so much pain that the overwhelming disappointment takes up residence deep inside us, causing a bitterness that keeps us from having an accurate perspective of any individual disappointment. This is the perfect setup for the beginning of self-destructive patterns.

Unlike simple disappointments, which occur during a short time period, complex disappointments develop over time. They begin with the same basic steps as simple disappointments.

Step One—We have deep roots of disappointment in our past. A complex disappointment usually begins with expectations from our childhood. Let's look at the evolution of Sarah's simple disappointment into a complex disappointment, which led to a major depression. When she was a young girl, Sarah's father continually disappointed her by breaking a promise of doing something special together because of his work. She may have been upset by her father's lack of commitment to her at the time, but her hurt quickly vanished in hope of the "next time." It was a simple disappointment.

However, with each year more simple disappointments were added (he didn't attend her school play, he forgot about the father-daughter banquet, and he even arrived late at her high school graduation), and she began to expect him to disappoint her. She learned to escape the hurt of her father's busyness and broken promises by imagining a dream marriage to a wonderful man who would always be emotionally available to her.

Larry, her first husband, seemed to be a charming man who was caring and thoughtful. In the early stages of their marriage, they sometimes stayed up into the wee hours of the morning just talking. Although he mainly expressed his love sexually, Sarah thought she had found someone who truly cared for her, someone who would not disappoint her—her dream man.

Step Two—We gradually realize the dream isn't coming true. After a few years Sarah started to notice that her Prince Charming wasn't so charming after all. Larry had begun a new, promising job and devoted most of his time and energy to his work. He traveled a lot, and when he wasn't traveling, he brought home stacks of work that "had to be done." If Sarah complained, Larry quickly pointed out that all these extra hours were necessary if they were to "get ahead and realize their dreams." Sarah told herself it was only temporary; after a promotion or two, things would change.

When Sarah became pregnant with their first child, they were both excited. Larry talked a lot about the baby, but after the baby was born, he worked the same long hours. Sarah was convinced that if she could make their home warm and inviting, and not demand anything of Larry, he would change his priorities. But no matter what she did, nothing ever changed. Gradually Sarah realized her dream of a close, warm, emotionally connected family was slipping away.

Step Three—We resist the growing awareness and simply try harder. If Larry wasn't turning out to be the husband Sarah had hoped for, then it must be her fault—she simply hadn't been all she could be. She would just have to work harder and put more time and energy into it.

Sarah's resistance followed a pattern. First, she attributed the problem to outside circumstances: It was the demands of Larry's job. It was the traveling he had to do. Next, she attributed the problem to herself: She wasn't being a good enough wife or homemaker. She needed to try harder. But the harder she tried, the more everything stayed the same.

Sarah also tried to keep her dream alive by controlling things. Everything in their home was well done and ran smoothly. The meals were tastefully prepared on time, and the kids were warned to be on their best behavior, especially if Dad was around. If Larry forgot to call and let her know he would be working late, Sarah would get angry, but she always tried to control it. Instead of yelling at him, she started to nag. When he didn't respond, she pressed harder. Finally Larry would pick a fight with her. They would exchange harsh words, and then both would retreat into silence for several days.

Sarah started looking around for help anywhere she could—she talked with her friends, comparing frustrations, she read all the self-help books on marriage she could find, she learned how to use "I" statements rather than accusatory phrases like "You did it." She became an expert at all the "helpful things" a wife could do to win her husband's approval.

During this stage, Sarah was denying the increasingly clear truth that nothing much was ever going to be different in her marriage. Acknowledging this truth would have meant a radical adjustment to her dreams. The more our perception of ourselves is based on our dreams, the longer we resist facing the reality of our situation.

One woman was very aware that she was clinging to her dream. "My life has always been full of fantasies. I had a fantasy about what kind of man my father was, and what kind of woman my mother was. I had a fantasy about what kind of man I would marry and what our life together would be like. I may not have much when my life doesn't measure up, but I still have my fantasies about what it should be."

(In Chapter 7 we will look at the many other ways we try harder to make our dream come true—and only make it worse.)

Step Four—Eventually the alarm goes off! Eventually, the reality of a situation becomes so obvious that we can no longer deny the truth. It's like a rude alarm that continues ringing and finally awakens us from our dream. Once we're awake, we can't deny the truth any longer. Sarah kept her dream alive through her first marriage, her divorce, her dating, and into her second marriage. It wasn't until her second marriage hit the twelfth anniversary mark—the time her first marriage had ended—that she began to experience the familiar emotional emptiness.

Some of us think we can put off the inevitable by hitting the snooze button when the alarm goes off. Change the lead characters in our dream and we won't have to wake up. Sarah, in effect, "fired" her first husband and then "hired" her second husband as her new "lead man." But when their life together didn't parallel the script of her dream, she could fool herself no longer.

Step Five: Our choice—disillusionment or disenchantment. When the alarm of reality goes off, we have a choice. Author William Bridges defines this choice as being the difference between being disillusioned and being disenchanted.[1]

Disillusionment allows us to go "back to sleep," to maintain our old point of view about life so we can meet our earlier unmet needs. And once we get back to "sleep," we can keep living in our dream world.

Disillusioned women hold on to their old dreams. Rather than moving forward with life, they stop and go through all the same old motions again. They are perpetually searching for the right husband or the real friend or the most fulfilling job. But no matter how drastic the changes, their dreams still don't come true.

Complex disappointments go much deeper than simple disappointments because the dream becomes part of a pattern of behaviors (our ways of manipulating our lives and the people in them to meet our unmet needs). When we fail to learn from our experiences, we become locked in a pattern of destructive behaviors that includes being disillusioned with the other people in our lives.

Prior to her counseling, Sarah blamed each failure on her choice of men and then went on and tried harder to make a better choice in the future. She never looked deep enough to see the pattern of her behavior, let alone what it meant in her life, so her choice or husbands always ended up the same.

As long as we fail to recognize the pattern of our behaviors and its meaning in our lives, we can cling to our dream and keep our lives status quo. By holding on so tightly to our dreams, we postpone the painful process of finding other ways to meet our unmet needs.

Disenchantment forces us to "wake up" from the fairy tale of our dreams and stay awake so we can look beneath the surface and see what is happening. It "breaks the spell" under which we have been operating. An example of disenchantment is our discovery as children that there is no Santa Claus. The magic of Santa Claus served us well as children, but at some point, we realized he was nothing more than make-believe and that all those people dressed up like him were just pretending. Other disenchantments include the discovery that parents make mistakes and even lie about it; that life really isn't fair; and that "I am not everything I think I am." None of these realizations are easy, but we must accept the new reality in order to begin the process of disenchantment.

Disenchantment means we face the truth that a part of our lives was lived in a dream, not in reality. When the spell is broken, the scales fall from our eyes, and we can begin to see the truth, maybe for the first time ever. We face our disappointments and learn the lessons they have to teach us about ourselves and life. Disenchantment looks deeper into our disappointments, a process we will outline in Part III. Disenchantment breaks the chain that binds us so we can dream different kinds of dreams—ones that can be fulfilled.

Personal Reflections:
Your Simple and Complex Disappointments

1. Review the disappointments you listed at the end of Chapter 3. See if you can identify the simple, or single-episode, disappointments and the more complex disappointments, which represent disappointments over time.

Simple Disappointments	Complex Disappointments
_____	_____
_____	_____
_____	_____

2. Now take one complex disappointment and try to chart its development.
   The complex disappointment Jan shared at the beginning of the chapter would look like this:

Unmet Needs: The attention and closeness I expected in childhood.

Childhood Dream: I would have a family that was close and who would share meaningful things around the table at holidays. My husband would take the lead in the sharing.

Adult Expectations: I expected Dave to take the lead without my needing to prompt him or do it for him.

Dream Doesn't Come True: He didn't do what he said he would do.

Disappointment: I can't trust him. My family will never have the special times I long to have with them.

Adult Behavior—Blame Others: I don't deal with my disappointment or with its roots. Instead, I blame Dave and think I can help him do it right the next time.

Hold on to the Dream: Next year it will be different.

Hurt Again: Next year probably won't be too different from this year.

   Now think about your own disappointment and the links in that cycle. Fill in your comments, as Jan did hers, below:

Unmet Needs: _____

_____

Childhood Dream: _____

_____

Adult Expectations: _____

_____

Dream Doesn't Come True: _____

_____

Disappointment: _____

_____

Adult Behavior—Blame Others: _____
_____

Hold on to the Dream: _____
_____

Hurt Again: _____
_____

And the cycle goes round and round, from disappointment to hurt to dreaming to disappointment. This cycle is an example of "trying harder." In the next chapter we will look at the many other ways in which we try harder to make our dream come true—and only make it worse. We call these coping mechanisms.

—7—

Trying Harder Only Makes It Worse

I always thought my husband and I would be facing our problems and disappointments together," said Carole, the woman whose husband has Huntington's Disease. "That's how it was ten years ago when Rich lost his job and was out of work for almost a year. We really hung together then. When I was discouraged, he pulled me up. When he was down, I was there for him. We prayed together, planned together, and assured each other that everything would be all right. But now that he is incapable of even carrying on a conversation with me, I'm facing all the problems alone. Life certainly isn't turning out the way I thought it would, and there is absolutely nothing I can do about it."

None of us wants to give up and simply accept what life throws at us. Henry Wadsworth Longfellow once wrote: "Tell me not, in mournful numbers, life is but an empty dream!" None of us wants to be told our lives are just empty dreams. In our surveys, we found that, in spite of the realities many women live with each day, most tenaciously cling to their dreams. To give up dreaming is almost to give up living. So how do we cope with the tremendous gap that can exist between our hopes and expectations, and the starkness of our reality?

When faced with complex disappointments, many of us turn to coping styles that only leave us grasping in the direction of our dreams. Even though these false solutions do nothing to change our reality, we stick with them, either because they allow us to stay in our dream mode or because they let us postpone facing the truth of our situations.

Carole's disappointments are many and complex, and they are threatening to push her into depression. And though she may not be able to do anything about the problems, she can choose how she responds to them. She can choose disenchantment (to wake up from the fairy tale of her dream) over disillusionment. But to do so, she will have to overcome the coping mechanisms that allow her to smother her pain.

COPING MECHANISMS

As we look at the following coping mechanisms, see if you can recognize any that you use regularly.

Just Grin and Bear It

Jan always believed: "If anything goes wrong, I have to try harder so it won't happen again. I must struggle to rise above this and smile and go on."

But should we try harder? Should we just accept our fate?

Busyness, or Doing for Doing's Sake!

Busyness is probably the most common way we have of avoiding the painful issues we face in our lives.

If we can just run fast enough and stay busy enough, surely we will be able to stay ahead of the disappointment.

We don't want to look at the cloud over us or even admit it is there. If we ignore it, maybe it will go away and things will get better.

"I coped by burying myself in my work," Carole told us. "No one could believe how much work I got done."

Work is only one of the ways of staying busy. Sometimes we stay busy with people. "What's wrong with that?" you may ask. "Doesn't most of the healing in our emotional lives take place in the context of relationships? If we want to effectively deal with our disappointments, don't we need people?" Certainly we do. The problem is, when we talk about busyness, we aren't talking about developing and building healthy relationships. Instead we are talking about being involved with other people just to stay busy.

An example is working hard at trying to help other people fix their own broken dreams. A young woman named Jessica described herself as a relationship addict, especially where men are concerned. "I sought refuge with boyfriends, hoping that a relationship would fix the deep ache within me," she told us. "In those relationships, I had to control everything. I had to know everything about my friends' lives. The focus was always on them. I had a whole pack of manipulation skills I had learned over the years, and I used them very subtly and tactfully to keep from ever having to talk about me." Should anyone start to show an interest in Jessica or in her life, she quickly changed the subject. To talk about herself would mean she would have to confront the disappointment again, and that is exactly what her busyness was attempting to avoid.

Marian told us she coped by trying to please everyone. "On the outside, I would just grin and bear it," she said. "I felt that if I just complied with what everyone else in my life wanted from me, it would eventually be my turn and they would take care of me. But it never was my turn. More and more I grew to resent the needs of others. But I couldn't face that, so I just stayed busy pleasing everyone else."

Like Carole, Marian turned her busyness to her workplace. "I would simply spend more time at work. My boss loved it. He was the only one who stayed at the office longer than I did. And then when I came home, there was always more to do than I had time for. So it was easy to stay busy. When I finally retired, I had too much time on my hands. I started to go crazy, so now I keep busy going to different support groups and seminars."

Another woman told us she coped by "reading every self-help book I could find, attending every seminar offered, and running from one support group to another. I was overwhelmed with busyness designed to fix me."

We have to wonder whether these women's support groups will help them successfully deal with their disappointments, or if they will simply become something else they can stay busy with to avoid the real pain inside.

Often these busy women described themselves as quiet and withdrawn within their families or at work. A big part of removing themselves from the disappointment was to clam up and say nothing while they kept on trying to fix everything. On the surface, they had an optimistic spirit about things, a spirit that reinforced the belief that "someday, sometime, my dream will come true. I just need to try harder!"

So, what's the big problem? Carole speaks for many when she said, "I keep going on, and I keep working and I keep doing. But more and more I resent everyone around me, and I get angrier and angrier at my husband." The problem is that we can only deny our hurt for so long before it eventually intrudes into our lives.

Before we actually become aware of our growing bitterness and resentment, we may begin to feel guilty about our own futile attempts to fix the situation. Inevitably we will end up believing that somehow we just aren't doing it right. This feeling of failure feeds right into our busy cycle of trying harder to fix the situation, which in turn gets us more of the same behaviors and frustrations we are trying so hard to fix.

Over time, trying harder can even cause physical illness. One woman said, "When I look at my disappointments, I've found that I have a strong tendency to turn on myself with anger and resentment until I finally make myself sick." Carole said, "My relentless busyness has brought on ulcers and migraine headaches." The irony is that illness in itself is a way of coping: When we end up sick, at least we have a face-saving way to stop trying.

If busyness is not your way of coping, you may be saying, "But it seems so futile to keep on trying!" Yet to the person holding on to the dream that things will get better, no other alternative makes sense. They have to keep on.

"I may be worn out, but staying busy does give me a sense of fulfillment," Carole said. Many women agree. Some even feel a sense of superiority about their efforts to fix themselves and their situations, at times even feeling "god-like" in their belief that only they can make a difference. Unfortunately, this unfounded sense of power gives nothing but a false sense of hope. True recovery always involves coming to terms with the truth, both within the situation and within oneself.

Pretending

The contradictory belief we mentioned in Chapter 6—"It is all my fault, and I just need to fix myself"—is just a short step away from taking on the task of making everything in life perfect. If everything were perfect, we think, then others would be delighted to play out the parts we expect of them, and our dreams would all come true. But everything isn't perfect, and keeping up the illusion means we have to keep on pretending everything is okay, even when we are overwhelmed with disappointment.

Rather than deal with who we really are, or with the truth about what exists around us, we create a pretend self and try to live up to it. The thinking goes like this: If I could just do it perfectly, or if I could be perfect, then all the love and closeness I desire, and every other one of my fantasies, will come true. In our striving to make "the idealized me" a reality, we work hard at traits like being nice or always being happy. I will be a spiritual giant, we promise ourselves, or I will stay young and thin, or I will never have a harsh word for anyone.

A person who copes this way has to be an awfully good pretender. She may pretend that the other person's behavior doesn't make any difference to her. She pretends that everything is okay. It has to be.

A number of wives stated that they coped with their husbands' unfaithfulness by pretending. One woman said, "When I try to talk about the hurts and disappointments, I am met with anger or denial, so I usually just go back to pretending that everything is okay. I can't live with things being unsettled. My husband has repented and asked for forgiveness from both God and me, but I just can't seem to get through it."

Husbands, as well as others in our lives with whom we are disappointed, are usually quite good at stonewalling our attempts to talk through our feelings of disappointment. Anger, silence, and picking a fight about some other subject are some of the defenses they use to shut us up. Eventually we get the message and pretend everything is fine.

"'You are so strong,'" Carole said. "That's what I hear from everyone." Striving for a perfectionism makes it look as if we have dealt with our hurts and disappointments, and this causes others to think everything is okay. And if everything is okay, they don't want to rock the boat. But underneath the surface, the longing is still there. "I don't feel strong," Carole said with a shade of bitterness. "Sometimes I wish they could see how scared and worn-out I am inside." But they can't, because Carole, like so many of us, stays busy making everything as perfect as possible in her struggle to keep her disappointments stuffed away.

Accepting

"There are lots of people who have had a much shorter, and much less successful and happy, life than Rich has," Carole said brightly. "And it's true for me, too. Sure, I've got problems, but there are lots of people who would envy my life. I have a lovely home. I have two wonderful kids."

Eventually, attempts to grin and bear it lead to passive submission. In order to settle for less than we had hoped and prayed for, we have to go through certain intellectual exercises designed to somehow make it acceptable. One of the most common intellectual games we play is minimizing what we have lost. Our motto becomes: "It really wasn't that important."

When we don't lose our dreams completely, we fall into what we've identified as the "M & M disease." This is our tendency to maximize one side of the issue and to minimize the other side. Women who suffer from this condition maximize their husbands' efforts—assuming he made some— and then minimize the importance of whatever the women had been hoping for from those efforts. Say, for example, that your husband has just forgotten your anniversary again. As you lie there in bed that evening feeling the disappointment, you begin to tell yourself such things as, "Yes, but he is a good provider. And he did remember my birthday this year." Then you minimize the hurt with thoughts like, "So what's an anniversary anyway? It's just another day in the year. I should be grateful he's still happy being married to me."

Another form of "M & M" is demonstrated by the woman who described her coping style this way: "Sometimes I try to think about why the disappointment happened, and then I try to think of the positive things about my disappointment. Usually I can find something positive, no matter what the disappointment is. Then I focus on that little bit of positiveness, and push away the problems and the reality of my situation."

Sometimes we "accept whatever" by taking a passive-submissive role and analyzing the situation again and again. Patricia said, "I will rehash the thoughts over and over and over in my mind. I've tried everything I can think of to understand why my husband had an affair. I've questioned him for three years now. I just can't get it out of my mind. I even had lunch with the other woman and asked her six pages of questions." What did this disappointed woman learn? That no answer satisfied her. Every one only led to more questions. Patricia's marriage may not survive, more because of her three years of questions than her husband's unfaithfulness!

When a woman plays this intellectual game, she tends to analyze every statement and action that has taken place, looking for any little nuance on which she can hang her continued hopes. Patricia continued, "I think that maybe, just maybe, I'll learn something from this disappointment that will help protect me in the future from ever having to experience it again. So I not only try to analyze why it happened, I carefully dissect every word and action taken by everyone, hoping to try and understand how I could have acted differently." Another woman commented on her tendency to analyze and rehash by saying, "I try to make it a learning experience, and then hope that I have learned the lesson so I won't have to 'repeat the class.'"

Sometimes our passivity leads us to a place of bitter acceptance. "I've gradually come to the place where I am accepting that this is all there is," was the way one woman put it. "I guess this is just my station in life." It takes a lot of rationalizing to come to this level of passivity.

Many people who use this type of coping add a spiritual dimension to their rationalizations. "After all," one woman said, "God is in charge, so if He wants me to suffer like this, I guess I can put up with it." Little wonder that some women felt that over the years they had developed the bitter feeling that even God had let them down.

EMOTIONAL SHUTDOWN

Once we adopt these intellectual coping mechanisms, we are treading on dangerous ground. We start to shut down our emotional responses as we turn up the volume on our intellectual responses.

What begins as minimizing the situation moves to rationalization over time. Eventually, as we numb ourselves to the pain, we become increasingly numb to all feelings, both good and bad. In the end we can become locked away inside ourselves, frozen emotionally, acting and talking normally on the outside but actually unable to connect with anyone.

Carole told us about a woman in her support group named Laura. "It's strange," Carole said, "when Laura starts talking, I begin to feel more and more tired and sleepy. It doesn't happen when others are talking, only Laura." Actually, it isn't so strange. Carole is responding to Laura's emotional deadness.

It's easy to criticize the Lauras in our lives. But what we must keep in mind is that the shutting down of emotions was caused by the pain those women were enduring, pain that was simply too much for them. Dying emotionally was their desperate means of survival.

Several other things accompany a shutdown of emotions:

1. An Uncanny Ability to Placate Everyone Around

Other people must be kept in a peaceful state, for if they get upset, it may stir up emotions within us that we don't want to face. The temptation is to become a chameleon, constantly adjusting to whatever we think others want us to be.

2. A Storytelling Ability

One woman said she coped by "submerging my feelings about the disappointment, and then talking about pleasant memories." Of course, talking about something pleasant isn't the same as experiencing it. That's why the stories don't quite ring true. Carole told us, "Laura never says anything negative, but she never sounds happy either." Because people who shut down emotionally can't tolerate negativity in themselves or in anyone else, their stories end up flat. There is no meaning to them. How can there be? Meaning in life comes through emotional connectedness with other people.

3. An Inner Void

Over time, if the meaninglessness of life continues to grow, we will eventually become aware of an inner void. Left to itself, this void will leave us in a profound state of despair and hopelessness.

GETTING FROM HERE TO THERE

You may be saying, "But that's not me! I'm not emotionally dead!" Neither is Carole. But unless she changes her track, she may be eventually. So what are the steps that lead from busyness to deadness?

Isolation

"I withdraw from the people in my life," Laura admitted, "even those who care about me and try to understand."

It makes sense to isolate ourselves from those who are hurting us. We withdraw to protect ourselves. But isolation goes far beyond simply pulling in for safety.

Women who responded to our survey said they "became inward, afraid to enter relationships of any kind." Some of them said, "I'm so insecure around others that it's easier to just withdraw." Several likened the withdrawal to "building a wall around myself." When we asked a group of women to describe a place that would feel safe for them, one said her safe place was a concrete tower.

"Were there any windows?" we asked.

"No," the woman said.

"Were there any doors?"

"No."

"How do you leave your safe place?" we asked.

"I never thought about that," the woman said. "I was only concerned that no one be able to intrude into my space. I guess in my desire for safety, I really isolated myself."

Laura insisted that although she may be withdrawn, her emotions are intact. "I still cry," she said. "Sometimes I even cry myself to sleep. So I am still feeling."

Maybe. But crying by yourself is also a way to stay detached emotionally, especially when the crying leads to sleep.

John Huston's movie *The Dead* is a wonderful example of emotional shutdown. In a scene near the end, the character played by Huston's daughter was with her husband in a hotel room, following an emotionally dead dinner party. As she talked with him, she suddenly had a very painful memory of something that had happened years ago when she was sixteen. She described a scene where her boyfriend came to visit her just before she was to leave for six months. Even though he was quite ill at the time, he braved severe weather to say good-bye to her in person. A week later he died. The woman began to weep as she told her husband how, over the years, she had continued to blame herself for his death.

The camera switched to her husband, who was standing by a window, listening jealously. "Did you love him?" he asked.

Emotionally, the woman was alone in that room. Her husband could neither understand her pain nor relate to her as she talked to him. Realizing this, she began to sob and sob, until she finally cried herself to sleep.

Crying alone has an uneasy quality; while it releases some internal tension, it also leads us right back into our deadness. Only when we can cry with someone who is emphatically able to connect with our pain is our crying therapeutic.

We Feed Ourselves

Chocolate and ice cream are Laura's solaces. "The more solace I need, the bigger the hot fudge sundae I make," she told her group.

There is an interesting connection between "stuffing" our feelings and "stuffing" our mouths. Many of us numb ourselves with food. Like Laura's enormous sundaes, food is often considered a comfort. And it's no wonder. When you were little and you fell down and hurt yourself, what did your mother do? She probably patched up your hurt, then gave you cookies and milk to help you feel better. It feels awfully good to be able to be mommy's little girl again. When life disappoints us, the one thing no one can take away is the comfort of eating.

"For years I stayed in denial about my disappointments," one woman explained. "I overworked myself and I overate. It started when I was young. As a seventh grader, I already weighed 207 pounds."

Overeating and bulimia were cited by women in our survey as common ways to numb themselves. "I used to handle my disappointments by drinking and binge-purging," Donna told us. "I stopped drinking, but I can't stop the binge-purge cycle."

In many ways, the binge-purge cycle of bulimia is like our disappointments. "When I sit down to eat something, I imagine how wonderful it is going to be," Donna continued. "But then I want so much of that goodness that I stuff myself. Then, when the food hits my stomach, I realize how disappointing it all was. Then I have to throw up and get rid of what I ate."

For women locked into this trap, the experience is both good and bad. When the food is in the store or on the table, it is all good. In fact, it is wonderful. "I can sit there and fantasize about how I am going to enjoy eating it," one woman told us. But once they start eating, such women can't stop. Eventually, they eat so much that what once was all-good now becomes all-bad, so they have to get rid of it.

Binge-purging takes over a person's life so completely that while she is involved in it, she is unaware of anything else. Afterwards, many of the women reported that they felt angry at themselves and terribly depressed. Interestingly, most didn't see the depression as related to the other issues in their lives. They only saw it as connected to the eating problem. "I am depressed," they said, "because of the way I eat."

Anorexia, too, can be a defense against feeling pain. One of the common dynamics here is the person's attempt to stop growing physically. There is a sense in which she wants to stay young and immature, hoping against hope that what she longs for will eventually come to her. Quite often, the underlying issues are related to a woman's disappointments with her father. Some theorists believe that she stops eating in the hope that she can get whatever she has missed from her father before she "grows up." One woman wrote, "I don't really handle my disappointments well. I have anorexia and bulimia, and I feel lonely and unworthy most of the time. My biggest disappointment has been feeling unloved and abandoned by my parents. I ended up spending a number of years living in foster homes."

How are eating disorders related to emotional deadness? Any activity that controls us is an attempt to numb ourselves. It is a distorted form of self-nurturing that makes other people unnecessary in our lives. It's as if the sufferer is saying, "Since I haven't found any other way to take care of my emotional needs, I'll take care of them through my eating." And so she eats herself into numbness.

Alcohol and drug abuse are also common ways women use to try to numb themselves. No one really knows how many women are addicted to alcohol or drugs, especially to prescription drugs. Because they seldom seek treatment, many remain a hidden part of our society, left to struggle with their problems alone.

"I never drink, and I certainly don't use drugs," Laura insisted. "I seldom even take aspirin!" But what she does do is watch soap operas nonstop. Television makes it easy to simply tune out the world and get lost in endless sitcoms. One woman told us, "In the evenings, I just 'veg-out' with the television. I watch anything that's on. If I go to bed and don't fall right to sleep, the quiet drives me crazy. My mind races over and over things I don't want to think about. So I usually fall asleep watching television."

When All Else Fails, We Dissociate

"I refuse to get involved in things that are going to bring me disappointment," Laura stated emphatically.

Other women we talked with were also adamant about cutting themselves off from anything that would lead to disappointment. They described their coping style as "dissociating" from the memory of the hurt or disappointment. To dissociate means "to disconnect or separate." It's a big step beyond denial, withdrawal, detachment, or even isolation. Dissociation is what happens when a woman cuts herself off from herself.

Here is how it starts: A person will often describe having "separated from myself and watched what was going on from a distance" sometime in the past. Later on, in situations that remind her of that earlier hurt, she will totally distance herself from what is going on around her.

"I often see myself completely separate, even from conversations I am involved in," one woman told us. "It's as if I am watching my own life like a movie."

Here's how Laura described it: "I disconnect from whoever and whatever is going on around me. Most of the things that have disappointed me over the years are simply blocked from my memory. I never even think about them anymore."

But dissociating does not resolve the issue. "Even though I don't remember much, I am very down on myself," Laura continued. "I always blame myself for anything that goes wrong. I abuse myself with overeating, and then I isolate myself. I guess the memories are still there someplace."

Carole is struggling between disillusionment and disenchantment. Laura has chosen disillusionment and has already crossed over into emotional deadness. She is cut off from everyone—even herself.

Personal Reflections:
Your Coping Mechanisms

Do you cope with problems by staying busy? By accepting your "fate"? Have you, like Laura, actually shut down emotionally? Perhaps the following exercise will help you understand more about yourself and your coping methods.

1. When you are disappointed, what do you do? Check the coping mechanisms that you are using:

_____ *Busyness*   _____ *Striving to be perfect*

_____ *Pretending*   _____ *Accepting your fate*

_____ *Trying to please others*   _____ *Maximizing/ Minimizing*

2. What do you tell yourself? _____

_____

_____

_____

3. Do you recognize any of the results of "emotional shutdown" in yourself? Check the ones below:

_____ *Rationalizing*   _____ *Storytelling*

_____ *Placating everyone*   _____ *A feeling of an inner void*

4. Describe any times you have shut down emotionally:

By eating: _____

_____

By isolating yourself: _____

_____

By using drugs or alcohol: _____

_____

By escaping through television: _____

_____

Gradually, as we shut down emotionally, we have an increasingly narrow experience of feelings. The feelings of hurt are small, but so are the feelings of joy. On the following scale, with 1 being emotionally dead and 10 being emotionally alive, rate your own emotional aliveness:

1—2—3—4—5—6—7—8—9—10
Emotional   Emotional
Deadness   Aliveness

Because we're seldom able to see ourselves truly objectively, talk with someone who knows you well to see if he or she agrees with your assessment.

We hope you have decided to give up your coping mechanisms after reading this chapter and completing the Personal Reflection. By choosing disenchantment (to wake up from the fairy tale of your dreams), you will have decided to break the chain of disappointment.

If you haven't made that choice, however, you will come up against the wall of depression, the final link in the chain of disappointment. We'll look at depression in Chapter 8.

—8—

The End of the Chain:
The Wall of Depression

E veryone knew why Cynthia was so depressed, yet no one knew what to do about it. Her husband, Jim, had finally left home and filed for a divorce. Cynthia and her friends knew this was not the first girlfriend he had had, just the one he thought he couldn't live without.

Over the course of eight years Cynthia had overlooked his late nights, his lame excuses, even his quick temper, which led him to "discipline" their children way beyond what was necessary. Instead of acknowledging her problem, she had busied herself taking classes in accounting at the local junior college, she had begun drinking and partying even more herself, and she had increased her chain smoking to four packs a day (the recent articles she read were right: Cigarettes were the perfect drug, a tranquilizer when she needed soothing, a pickup when she needed energy).

Cynthia did not choose disenchantment (to wake up from the fairy tale of her dream world). Instead, she continued to fool herself until Jim broke her reverie. Now she had to face both the reality of Jim's desertion and the fact that his behavior had been going on for years. That made her so angry that she simply shut down. She seldom went outside of the house, and she never got up until lunchtime or later. She stayed up late into the night reading or watching whatever movie seemed halfway interesting.

Eventually, when complex disappointments become overwhelming, women encounter their anger, no matter how much they have tried to numb themselves against the pain. But this anger is rage, not healthy anger that will help them process their losses and grieve. This sort of anger is designed to push people away, which is the type of anger men frequently express.

DISAPPOINTED WOMEN: ANGRY MEN

If we were to ask a group of men about their disappointments, the question would probably confuse them. "Who has time for such things?" would be a typical response. Men don't talk about their disappointments as women do.

It isn't that men aren't disappointed; it's just that their response to disappointment is generally quite different from that of a woman. As Tim Allen, the tool man of the popular television program "Home Improvement," says, "Women respond by manipulating; men respond by blowing up bridges." The few men who would admit to being disappointed would see themselves as having a more active role in trying to "fix" the thing that caused their disappointment than women do.

Several years ago, Dave, along with Stephen Arterburn, wrote a book called *The Angry Man*. In doing the research for that book, they found that men generally cover up their disappointments with anger. And anger causes them to take some aggressive action, which may not be productive or wise; they may blow up bridges! Women, on the other hand, turn their anger inward.

This response is not all that surprising, since our culture teaches women to respond differently than men. As Colette Dowling pointed out in *The Cinderella Complex*, little boys are trained to move out of dependency on other people in order to become independent, whereas little girls are trained into dependency.[1] Although men and women are innately different (they are wired differently, you might say, by their genes), many of the differences are the result of cultural influences.

LITTLE BOYS HAVE PERMISSION TO BE ANGRY

When men were little boys, it was more socially acceptable for them to show anger than it was for little girls. And when men become adults, it still is. Anger may be acceptable for little boys, but many other emotions, especially those associated with sadness, are not. "Stop those tears and act like a man," parents or coaches tell little boys when they strike out with the bases loaded in the Little League play-offs.

On the other hand, if a little boy gets angry and kicks the dirt or slams his bat to the ground, his parents or coach may even feel a little proud that he handled the disappointment "like a man." After all, that's probably what Dad would do if he struck out in his softball game.

Over the years boys are taught, both by family and by social pressures, "It's okay to be angry." "It's manly." On the other hand, it is not "manly" to be disappointed—to feel hurt, frustrated, or sad. Of course, some men, as well as some women, were taught that it is unacceptable, or even unsafe, to express any emotion, even anger, so they repressed all their emotions.

Men can't cry. And women can't be angry.

LITTLE GIRLS SHOULDN'T SHOW ANGER

The taboo against women displaying anger goes back to ancient times. Some of the first written laws, dating around 2500 B.C., penalized women for being verbally angry with their husbands. In one case, the punishment was to have a woman's name engraved on a brick, which was then used to knock out her teeth!

Over the centuries, our penalties have become a little more civil, but our attitudes haven't changed all that much.

Little girls are usually taught "It isn't ladylike to be angry." One woman was consistently given this message as a little girl: "If something doesn't go the way you want it to go, smile and act like nothing is wrong." She said, "Later I learned that when I was alone, or with a close girlfriend, I could express my anger, but even then, I knew I had to keep it under control."

Little girls are taught "It's not okay to be angry" but "It is okay to cry." The message is loud and clear: "Cover up your anger with disappointment and tears."

And that solution becomes a pattern that follows women into their marriages. One woman told us, "When I'm upset with my husband, I often tell myself, 'I'll wait until a better time to talk to him about this,' and of course there never is a better time. Or I think to myself, 'I don't want to upset things. I just want to keep everyone happy. What I'm feeling doesn't matter that much.'" In both cases, this woman avoids dealing with her anger and, more important, with the issues that caused her feelings.

Basically, women deny their anger because they are afraid: "If I don't hide my anger, I will alienate my husband (or children or friends or coworkers) and lose what little of them I may have." Instead, they express their disappointment by nagging or crying, as Jan's mother did in private, and try to make the best of things. Or by saying, "I'm bothered by. . . " or "I feel upset about . . . ."

Unfortunately, women still feel dependent in their relationships, and the more they think they need the other person, the less they are able to express any negative emotions. Cynthia, the woman whose husband left her after several affairs, told us, "I knew my husband had been unfaithful for several years, but I was afraid. I never worked after college. I don't know how to make a living for myself. I was afraid of what would happen to me and the girls if Jim left home."

A woman in our survey expressed the same fear: "I'm afraid to let my husband know how I really feel. I don't think our relationship could survive such honesty." Does this mean that women are actually less angry then men? Not at all.

BUT WOMEN ARE ANGRY!

Fatigue, embarrassment, frustration, rejection—all cause women to be angry, according to Dr. James Dobson in *Emotions—Can You Trust Them?* but still women were hesitant to identify their feelings as anger.[2] Yet counselors usually report that once women get in touch with their anger, they are angrier and more willing to honestly express it than men. And when that anger surfaces it is often directed at . . . you guessed it: men and, more precisely, husbands.

According to the survey Dave and Steve Arterburn conducted for the book, *The Angry Man,* men didn't focus their anger on their spouses.[3] They also didn't express as much discontentment with the way their lives were turning out. Perhaps men are so shut off from what they really feel that the anger they do express is simply a defense, designed to keep themselves and others at a distance from their real hurts or feelings of disappointment.

We see this dynamic at work in our relationship. At a certain point in an argument—usually when Dave realizes his reasoning is not well supported—he gets angry and leaves the room. At other times he becomes more insistent and dogmatic, staying with the argument, fiercely protecting his real hurt feelings. After years of hitting each other head-on, Jan has learned to stop talking and recognize his anger as his way to cover his hurt feelings. And Dave says, "I have learned to hear out Jan's disappointments, validate her underlying anger, and not try to fix them. Trying to change them only intensifies the anger I hide deep inside."

Again, women do experience anger, even though they may not be aware of it or call it anger. "We prove we are angry by the fact that we want revenge, much more so than men—we get even when we feel frustrated or helpless," Jan says. "Many times, we are confronted with our helplessness in the situation and the intense frustration we have felt over the years as we have tried to change things. That makes us angry, whether we admit it or not."

THE EXPRESSION OF ANGER

When we are hurt, frustrated, or injured in some way emotionally, it is natural to feel angry about what has happened. "The human body is equipped with an automatic defensive system, called the 'flight or fight' mechanism, which prepares the entire organism for action," says Dr. James Dobson. The "fight" part of that mechanism is anger, and "this is an involuntary response which occurs whether or not we will it."[4]

Our emotions are designed by God in such a way that anger results when we are hurt, especially when the hurt reminds us of an emotional injury from the past. It is the kind of anger Paul referred to when he said, "Be angry, and do not sin" (Eph. 4:26). The purpose of anger is to protect us, and it is a natural and healthy emotion—when it is expressed without sin. "Anger is simply a physical state of readiness," says psychologist Neil Clark Warren in his book, *Make Anger Your Ally.* "When we are angry, we are prepared to act. This is all anger is—preparedness."[5]

Unfortunately, both men and women react with defensive anger before they get to this pure, healthy anger.

The Ways We Express Our Anger

We often express our anger defensively, which is the most destructive way. Such anger leads us through a progression of four steps, which can end in bitterness and then lead to depression.

1. Emotional Outbursts Often we first express our anger as loudly as possible, which is a desperate attempt to get the attention of whoever is blocking our dream. This is pure defensive anger; we're defending ourselves against the hurt we feel so deeply. The women in our survey listed "yelling, raging, pouting, and whining" as common ways they expressed their anger once it came to the surface. Of course, the yelling would often be accompanied by tears. One woman said she did all these things in hopes that "it would shame my husband into caring."

Unfortunately, defensive anger seldom changes another person's attitude for the better. We yell, they yell back, and the war has begun. We know this, but we do it over and over again because a part of us still believes we can coerce this person into acting the way we want him or her to act. Eventually, we become so frustrated that we unconsciously decide to "get even."

2. Getting Even Several women listed their ways of "getting even," especially with their husbands, on their questionnaires: shopping or sabotaging something important to their spouse headed the list. These women said, "I kept score." Looking back, they were able to see that they kept track of their disappointments, and when "the score hit a certain mark," they felt entitled to buy something extravagant for themselves. They found their anger eliminated any immediate feelings of guilt. However, later some of these women couldn't really enjoy what they had bought because it reminded them of the emotional price of their purchases. Other women wore their purchase proudly, feeling they had more than "earned" it.

Women also mentioned forgetting to do something, like "take his suits to the cleaners" or being busy with the children or not feeling well or having car problems as ways they "got even." Still others listed, "Just being late, or making my husband late."

3. Blaming Someone Else Often we may be afraid to direct our anger at the person who has caused our disappointment because doing so would make it even more difficult to get what we desire. Instead, we find ourselves becoming short with our children, snapping at a sales clerk, yelling at someone in another car on the freeway, or in some other way displacing our anger and "kicking the dog."

Sometimes we substitute our original disappointment for a new disappointment with this neutral party. For example, when I am displacing my anger on my children, I actually believe that I am disappointed with their behavior. But the truth is, rather than confront the real disappointment within me, I now displace all this churning anger inside of me at my child, who may deserve my displeasure, but not to that extent.

4. Blaming Ourselves We're back to that same contradictory cycle of blaming others and blaming ourselves. When women first turn their anger inward, they somehow continue to appear to be very "nice" and "ladylike." Eventually, all sense of needing to be "nice" is gone; the disappointment becomes so overwhelming, the woman doesn't care anymore—she shows her anger! Now she doesn't care who sees it.

Carrie described how she started to lash out at her husband because of her disappointment with their lack of emotional closeness. As she lashed out, he simply reacted with his own defensive anger. Their story is all too common—their anger grew as the threats grew, and divorce became a part of the threats. Finally one moved out and the other filed for divorce.

As we talked with her later, Carrie told us how bitter the divorce was. She and her husband fought the whole way through it, but when they met to sign the final papers, they looked at each other with a feeling of longing, coupled with a sense of resignation. "I didn't want to divorce him, and I don't think he wanted to divorce me," she added. "When I said something like that to him, for a fleeting moment I thought he might soften, but then he said, 'We've come this far, I guess we should finish it.' I never really wanted a divorce—I just wanted him to hear me." Her out-of-control, defensive anger led her down a path she didn't want to travel.

Eventually, we turn all our anger and hatred onto ourselves and begin to act out our self-hatred in self-destructive behaviors. One woman said, "I've had affairs. I've had a drinking problem. I've abused credit by spending too much; I owe so much right now that the only way out is to declare bankruptcy. Most of the time I'm just angry with myself."

As she talked about her struggle, she commented on how often she seemed to create a crisis in her life. "I don't consciously plan to have a crisis, but I've had enough of them that it seems to be a pattern with me," she continued. "I think when I'm in the midst of a crisis I don't have to face my disappointments."

Eventually, self-hatred leads us to bitterness.

BITTERNESS, THE ANGER OF THE SOUL

Bitterness is a poison that destroys us, affects our families, and even infects those around us; bitterness leads to depression. The writer of Hebrews warns us to be careful, for "there can spring up. . . . a bitter spirit which is not only bad in itself, but can poison the lives of many others" (Heb. 12:15, J.B. PHILLIPS).

The Greek root for the word *bitterness* includes the meaning "to cut, to prick." Disappointment punctures our heart and eventually penetrates until it totally infects us and ends up defining who we are. A second definition of bitterness includes the idea of "intense hostility" toward someone. We feel alienated and estranged from people and take on a disagreeable, cynical attitude toward life.

Bitterness also affects our health. The Medical School of Duke University recently identified the number one killer in American culture as unforgiveness, the repressed anger we hold locked within ourselves. Chronic fatigue, hives and other skin disorders, cancer, irritable bowel syndrome, PMS, the common cold, and especially headaches are being identified as having a connection to repressed anger.

After Jim left Cynthia, the bad backaches that had plagued her for years increased; she had been diagnosed with a slightly ruptured disc, but the doctors said the damage shouldn't be producing so much pain. Cynthia spent several months in bed, treating her back with cold compresses and her pain with medication. Then finally she was able to resume her normal activities. She went back to

school to get more credits toward an accounting degree . . .
until she found the lump in her breast.

The doctors said the lump was malignant, so her breast
was removed, and Cynthia tried to overcome her loss—and
her fear that no man would ever love her now. Four years
later, just when she had decided to have reconstructive surgery on the first breast, a lump was found in the other
breast (a mirror image of the first cancer, but apparently not
a metastasis). Was the cancer exacerbated by Cynthia's bitterness? No one even raised the question in her case; what
would it matter anyway? Bitterness can destroy.

Many of the steps of bitterness are the same as the stages
of defensive anger, just on a much deeper level. We continue to play the victim, and we continue to complain about
our disappointments and nurse them in our hearts.

The Complaining Stage

Once we become bitter we are often willing to express
our feelings of hurt and disappointment to anyone who will
listen. Job experienced this when he said, "Therefore I will
not restrain my mouth; / I will speak in the anguish of my
spirit; / I will complain in the bitterness of my soul" (Job
7:11). As Job talks and talks about his anguish, he experiences what we experience; he ends up feeding the roots of
bitterness within himself.

Cynthia told us, "I used to talk for hours about my disappointments and hurt, but I never listened to what others
were saying to me. I just needed to talk. Eventually it became a way of life for me."

One of Cynthia's friends finally confronted her about her
constant complaining. "When she told me I seemed to
always be stuck in the same place, she got my attention. I
didn't want to hear what she was saying to me, but she per-
sisted until I did."

When we complain about our pain to someone else, we both become mere observers of the dreadful situation. It was easier for Cynthia to talk about her complaints than to do something about her disappointments.

The Nursing Stage

The next step along the path of bitterness is to pull back within ourselves. This stage is called the nursing stage, or the stage of quiet resentment. Now we say less, except within the privacy of our minds. We experience the truth of the proverb that says: "The heart knows its own bitterness, / And a stranger does not share its joy" (Prov. 14:10).

What an interesting combination of words—joy and bitterness. There is a morbid enjoyment in nursing our hurt and anger, massaging them as we bury them inside ourselves. Eventually bitterness feeds upon bitterness. Cynthia moved into the nursing stage after her friend confronted her with her constant complaining. "At first I wanted to stay in bed and pull the covers over my life. I simply shut up—I quit talking about my problems and most everything else as well.

"Fortunately, my friend knew what I was doing and she kept after me to get help. I found that just talking didn't do anything—neither did not talking. It took a different kind of talking for me to break the cycle."

Cynthia had learned the difference between complaining about her problems and sharing her emotions. When we really talk about how we feel, we are connected to our pain, and we are able to work our way through it to wholeness. Sharing our hurt with someone is always a part of our healing, but bitterness grows out of our complaining.

A spirit of bitterness that is nursed over a period of time eventually leads us into a place of isolation. An example of someone walking this path was Saul, Israel's first king. Soon after we meet Saul, we find him facing a seemingly unresolvable situation. The Philistines, the enemy of Israel, had a giant named Goliath, who paralyzed the Israelite army. The story of how David killed Goliath is well known. The less obvious story is Saul's growing resentment and bitterness at the glory David received for this feat.

After the miraculous defeat of Goliath (and several others), the crowds sang the following song as Saul and David passed by:

> "Saul has slain his thousands,
> And David his ten thousands."
> (1 Sam. 18:7)

Saul resented the words. His thousands were obviously outdone by David's ten thousands. Would David someday replace him? Saul worried. The possible answer enraged him.

Instead of working through his anger, Saul chose the path of bitterness. Later, "Saul eyed David from that day forward" (1 Sam. 18:9). Or we might say, "Saul nursed his anger in the quietness of his heart."

Over time, David became the close friend of Saul's son, Jonathan. David married Saul's daughter, Michal. Even his family seemed to prefer David, Saul thought. Finally his bitterness became so great, he told his servants and Jonathan to kill David.

Jonathan protested. Why kill someone who has meant you no harm and has even helped you in any way he could? The first time Jonathan protested, Saul listened, but he still nursed his bitterness. The second time Jonathan defended David from Saul's threats to kill him, the king's anger turned against his own son and he almost killed Jonathan. Later, when Saul's daughter, Michal, also tried to protect her husband, Saul gave her to another man specifically to spite David. All of Saul's behaviors were controlled by his irrational passion and bitterness. Eventually, Saul ended up a bitter and lonely man, destroying not only himself, but also those he loved as the walls of bitterness he had built over the years collapsed upon him.

THE DEAD END OF DEPRESSION

Just as it was in Saul's case, so it will be in ours—the years of defensive anger and bitterness will lead us into the pit of a paralyzing depression. Once we turn on ourselves with our anger, the path ahead is going to be even more rocky and painful. We've gradually withdrawn from those around us, cutting ourselves off from friends and support systems.

Depression Defined

A simple definition of *depression* is "a condition of general emotional dejection and withdrawal; sadness greater and more prolonged than that warranted by any objective reason."[6] Depression can encompass a wide range of emotions, along with feelings of helplessness, and these emotions do not move along a predictable, continuous path, from the "blues" to a more serious depression and finally to suicide. Instead, our experience of depression can vary.

Counselors use the *Diagnostic and Statistical Manual of Mental Disorders* (commonly referred to as the DSM-III-R) as our guide to diagnosis. The DSM-III-R lists fifteen different types of depression, most of them under the heading of mood disorders. Some are organically or biochemically based, but most result from unresolved issues and conflicts in our lives, both past and present.

One woman described her depression to us in this way. "The despair I'd been feeling over my life and all its disappointments became depression. My energy level was lower, my ability to concentrate was diminished, and my self-hate grew stronger as I saw myself as worthless. . . . I ate out of boredom and my weight shot up. I ended up feeling an extraordinary amount of guilt, and my ability to sleep was changed, adding to the feelings of fatigue I was already struggling with." Her description could be typical of a major depression, depending on how long she had been experiencing these symptoms and how severely they affected her ability to function on a daily basis.

Barbara Minar described these feelings as "The Depression Vulture [who] flapped so close I could feel the wind from his wings." Later, when he landed, she said, "A putrid smell hit my senses as I felt the Depression Vulture land in my emotions."[7] At any given time, more than seven million women in our country experience a major depression. This does not include those who are plagued by milder forms of depressive mood disorders, which are estimated to affect 20 to 25 percent of women. Studies have shown that women are twice as likely to be depressed as men are.

A study published by the American Psychological Association explained why. The higher proportion of women suffering from depression is, in many cases, directly related to women's tendency toward "certain cognitive and personality styles—avoidant, passive, dependent behavior patterns; pessimistic, negative cognitive styles; and focusing too much on depressed feelings instead of action and mastery strategies."[8]

Another study by M. Notman, in 1986, and quoted by Ellen McGrath, pointed out other factors that make women more vulnerable to depression than men.[9] These included differences in the attachment and separation process between boys and girls during early development (those old cultural myths that boys are to be independent, girls dependent), social stereotypes that devalue women in general, and the relatively fewer avenues available to women for activities and the mastery of those activities. Cynthia realized this when she told us she didn't feel equipped to support her girls and herself. "It will be different for my girls," she said. "Women now are supposed to develop their own potential; they often expect to have careers, rather than seeing themselves only as wives and mothers. I think my girls will stand up for themselves more than I did."

Additional factors include the fact that marriage provides a greater advantage for men than for women—that is, they are more easily satisfied and seldom refer to their marriages in negative terms. Women are more vulnerable. "In unhappy marriages, women are three times as likely as men to be depressed than married men and single women."[10]

Women today suffer from depression ten times more than their grandmothers did. Part of this increase is due to their higher expectations and the resulting long-term disappointments that haven't been processed.

The symptoms of depression identified in the DSM-III-R include a loss of interest in pleasurable activities most of the day and nearly every day; significant changes in weight (either losing weight or gaining weight); problems sleeping (either sleeping too much, too little, or awakening in the middle of the night and not being able to go back to sleep); either a slowing of movements or an observable agitation; a loss of energy; feelings of worthlessness; and difficulty concentrating.

Depression appears to be a very inactive state but, in fact, is a very active one. To an observer, depressed people appear immobilized. In reality, their minds are in a frenzy. They cannot function, but internally, they are despising themselves for it.[11]

Other symptoms expressed by women caught in the depressive cycle of their disappointments included experiences of anxiety and panic; sexual difficulties, including frigidity; the inability to trust anyone; a sense of depersonalization, which is experienced as a feeling of detachment from oneself; and the emotional deadness we described in the last chapter.

(If you identify with five or more of these symptoms, talk to your doctor about what you are feeling. There is help for depression, even though you may feel as though everything is hopeless.)

Unfortunately, most depressed women do not seek treatment for their depression, since they feel depression is a sign of weakness. Thoughts like "If only I were stronger, I wouldn't feel like this" or "I just need to discipline myself more to get things done" or "All I need is some rest or a break from the kids" keep them from seeking professional help. Yet a lack of treatment usually leads to a progressive worsening of the problem.

Several women reported that in their despair, they attempted to take their own lives. When we are emotionally dead, our self-hatred grows. We can see no way out of the deepening despair and depression. And our thinking becomes distorted as we isolate ourselves from others, so we often look for a quick way out of the pain. One woman told us, "I learned how to handle the smaller disappointments in my life and move on. But I couldn't see any way I could deal with the pain of my dad's sexual abuse. I've tried to kill myself several times."

Another woman said that she had been forced to slow down the pace of her life because of losing her job. "I overdosed on pills three times last year." When we are spiraling downward in depression, suicide may seem a logical next step.

Depression Caused by Disappointment

A series of experiments done during the nineteenth century by Paul Moebius, a German neuropathologist, illustrates how the frustration of our unfulfilled dreams, and subsequent disappointments, become depression. Moebius would often use experiments involving a pike fish that was swimming in a huge tank with glass walls to introduce the study of psychology to his medical students. The professor would throw a sturgeon fish into the tank, and the pike would immediately eat it.

Eventually, Moebius would put a strong glass partition in the tank, dividing it into two sections. Now he would throw in the sturgeon on the opposite side of the tank from where the pike was swimming. Following its natural bent, the pike would rush toward the small fish, only to slam into the glass and fall to the bottom stunned. As soon as the pike "got his senses back" it would dive toward the sturgeon again, only to hit the glass again.

Finally the professor would remove the glass plate, and the pike would swim around the sturgeon without any attempt to devour it. Sometimes the pike would get hungry enough to try again, and this time successfully enjoy a meal, while other times, the pike would never touch the sturgeon and "give up" on life.[12]

This pike experienced the same disillusionment that we experience when we have "butted our heads against the wall" in our expectations of husbands, family members, parents, or even life itself. Eventually we give up trying to get what we've dreamed of having, and in doing so, we give up on the people in our lives and lose any sense of joy in living—we are depressed.

This hopeless cycle looks something like the chart on page 147.

You'll notice that wall at the end of the spiral, the dead end of depression. This experience of depression is often described as being stuck or as being caught in a box canyon. There is no place to go when we get there! We either keep hitting our head against the wall or we simply lie down and give up.

The Chain of Disappointment

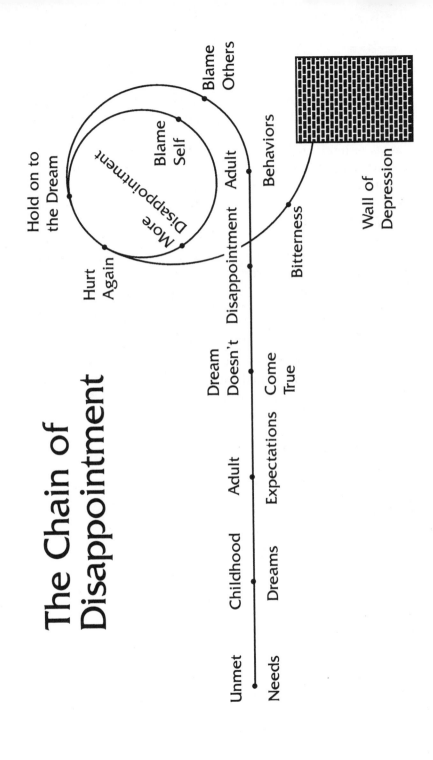

Unmet Needs — Childhood Dreams — Adult Expectations — Dream Doesn't Come True — Disappointment — Bitterness — Behaviors — Adult — Blame Self — More Disappointment — Hurt Again — Hold on to the Dream — Blame Others

Wall of Depression

No one wants to experience emotional pain. It is not a feeling we welcome or embrace. But when we fail to deal with emotional hurts and losses, either by pushing them away with our anger (as men tend to do) or by trying to bury them and becoming overwhelmed by disappointments and depression (as women generally do), the resulting emotional experiences will become more painful than dealing with the original issues.

Yes, we will find a lot of healthy anger underneath the surface. This can be frightening for us, but it can frighten the men in our lives even more. A colleague of ours commented some years ago, "One day women are going to find out how angry they really are, and then we men are going to be in real trouble!"

Perhaps there will be some temporary trouble for men as women get in touch with their anger, but the ultimate goal in looking at the anger hidden beneath our disappointments is to develop a greater capacity for love. With that as our goal, both men and women will win—it's worth the journey.

Personal Reflections:
Uncovering Your Healthy Anger

As you've read about the disappointments other women experienced, you may have found that you became angry for them, taking offense on their behalf. Sometimes that is the first step in acknowledging your own anger (it is easier to be angry for someone other than yourself).

Neil Clark Warren wrote in Make Anger Your Ally: "Anger is the coiling of the spring in you, an intricately designed internal process which gives you the capacity to manage the difficult and threatening parts of your life."[13]

Harriet Lerner voiced the same opinion in The Dance of Anger: "Anger is a signal, and one worth listening to."[14]

Note which disappointments stirred something within you. How does that particular disappointment relate to your own life?

As you begin to identify with these disappointments, you may begin to experience feelings of anger at your own disappointments. Don't be afraid of your angry feelings. Recognize that any anger you may be feeling is a signpost that points to some important information in your life.

Use the questions below to help you find your own healthy anger, for it provides the energy, the springboard, to see you through the process to wholeness.

1. What were you taught about anger as a little girl?

I learned from my father that anger _____

_____

I learned from my mother that anger _____

_____

I learned from my siblings that anger _____

_____

I learned from others outside of my family that anger _____

_____

2. What I learned as a child about anger causes me to (stuff my anger or let it explode, for instance)

_____

3. Do you see any difference in the way you express anger with men as opposed to how you express it with women? If so, how?

I express anger in the presence of men by _____

_____

I express anger in the presence of women by _____

_____

4. Do you see any difference in the way you express anger with the members of your immediate family as opposed to how you express it to other people? If so, how?

I express my anger with my family by _____
_____

I express my anger with others by _____
_____

5. Who in your family had permission to get angry?

It always seemed okay for _____ to get angry.

It was _____ who gave him or her permission to get angry.

6. How did this person express his or her anger?

_____ showed his or her anger by
_____

7. In what situations do you give yourself permission to get angry?

I get angry and show it when _____

8. If you are aware of your own anger, when did you become aware of it?

I became aware of my anger when (for example: I hit my daughter for little reason.) _____

It was _____ that triggered my anger in this situation.

9. *Has your anger led you to bitterness and then to depression?*
Check the symptoms of depression you have experienced at times:

_____ *loss of interest in pleasurable activities*

_____ *significant change in weight*

_____ *problems sleeping*

_____ *sleeping too much*

_____ *awakening in the middle of the night and not being able to go back to sleep*

_____ *a slowing of your movements*

_____ *your movements seem agitated*

_____ *a loss of energy*

_____ *a feeling of worthlessness*

_____ *difficulty concentrating*

_____ *feeling anxious or panicked*

_____ *sexual difficulties (including frigidity)*

_____ *the inability to trust anyone*

_____ *feeling detached from yourself and others*

10. *Check the ones you are experiencing right now:*

_____ *loss of interest in pleasurable activities*

_____ *significant change in weight*

_____ *problems sleeping*

_____ *sleeping too much*

_____ *awakening in the middle of the night and not being able to go back to sleep*

_____ a slowing of your movements

_____ your movements seem agitated

_____ a loss of energy

_____ a feeling of worthlessness

_____ difficulty concentrating

_____ feeling anxious or panicked

_____ sexual difficulties (including frigidity)

_____ the inability to trust anyone

_____ feeling detached from yourself and others

11. *If you are experiencing five or more symptoms now, what steps are you taking to get help for your depression?*

- _____

- _____

- _____

The good news is that you don't have to continue to butt your head against the wall of depression (in fact, if you chose to give up your coping mechanisms at the end of the last chapter, you won't experience a severe depression). You can always choose disenchantment (to wake up from the fairy tale of your dream).

You can say goodbye to your disappointments. You can find hope when your dreams don't come true. You can move from depression to a new hope. We will show you how in Part III.

— PART III —

From Depression to a New Hope: The Joy of Fulfillment

—9—

Climbing out of the Pit

T he following poem by Portia Nelson, entitled "Autobiography in Five Short Chapters," is often used in recovery groups:

I.

I walk down the street.
>There is a deep hole in the sidewalk.
>I fall in
>I am lost . . . I am helpless
>>It isn't my fault.

It takes forever to find a way out.

II.

I walk down the same street.
>There is a deep hole in the sidewalk.
>I pretend I don't see it.
>I fall in again.

I can't believe I am in the same place,
>>but, it isn't my fault.

It still takes a long time to get out.

III.
I walk down the same street.
   There is a deep hole in the sidewalk.
   I see it is there.
   I still fall in . . . it's a habit.
      My eyes are open.
      I know where I am.
It is my fault.
I get out immediately.

IV.
I walk down the same street.
   There is a deep hole in the sidewalk.
   I walk around it.

V.
I walk down another street.

We can get out of our holes. We can become disenchanted. Even better, we can learn to walk down different streets.

PREPARING FOR THE ASCENT

If we are to break the cycle of disappointment, we must begin to grieve over our losses. Grieving helps us come to a place where we can accept the truth, which includes the limitations that exist in our present life situations.

Chuck Swindoll is adamant about living his life in reality: "I would much prefer to live my life on the sharp, cutting edge of reality than dreaming on the soft, phony mattress of fantasy. Reality is the tempered poker that keeps the fires alive . . . it's the spark that prompts the engine to keep running . . . the hard set of facts that refuses to let feeling overrule logic. It's reality that forces every Alice out of her Wonderland and into God's wonderful plan. Its undaunted determination has pulled many a wanderer lost in the maze of meanderings back to the real world of right and wrong, the false and the true. Reality, I remind you, is the world from which most every emotionally—and mentally—disturbed patient has escaped—and the point to which they must return before health is restored. Hard as it may be to bear, it brings a practical security second to none. It is, unquestionably, the healthiest place on earth."[1]

Yes, reality is the healthiest place on earth. As comedienne Lily Tomlin says, "The best mind-altering drug is truth."

This shift in our usual cycle, however, requires us to do some very difficult things. For starters, it means we must accept the limitations of our spouses, our parents, our children, ourselves. No wonder it's not something we are eager to do. Yet facing the truth, and grieving over the gap that exists between that truth and our dearly held dreams, does lead to a place of acceptance. And out of the acceptance, we can learn to dream again. Only now, our mended dreams will be based on a reality that will allow that to come true.

"I'm not all that sure that facing reality will be good for me," said Carole, the woman whose husband is suffering from Huntington's Disease. "My reality is too depressing."

In her book *When Feeling Bad Is Good*, Psychologist Ellen McGrath differentiates between what she calls "healthy depression" and "unhealthy depression." Healthy depression is "based on realistic feelings of pain, sadness, and disappointment (accompanied at times by guilt, anger, and/or anxiety) from negative experiences." Unhealthy depression, on the other hand, is based on distortions of reality, including delusion and fantasy. If Carole is going to process her disappointments, she must deal with her reality. And if we are going to process *our* disappointments, we must deal with *our* reality.

Every one of us needs to find that place of healing we must create for ourselves in order to come to the place where we can say goodbye to our disappointments and find fulfillment in our lives. This process involves four steps: establishing a support system, grieving our hurts and losses, walking through the grieving process, and sharing our sadness and grief.

1. Establish a Support System

"Long before there was a medical diagnosis, I knew something was wrong with my husband," said Carole. "But the approach I had learned in childhood was to keep a smile on my face and any private problems tucked away inside me. Complaining was a sign of weakness. So I never said a word to anyone. When the diagnosis was made and we were given the gloomy prognosis, my husband warned me to keep it quiet. The pressure of having to keep it all inside me and pretend there was nothing wrong was horrible. Since Rich refused to accept the severity of his disease, I couldn't even talk to him."

Many times, when we come face to face with disappointment, the last thing we want to do is allow another person into that painful part of our lives. So we isolate ourselves and bar the door. We have seen how this feeds right into the cycle of despair and hopelessness. Research has consistently shown the importance of relationships as a context for healing.

Unfortunately, not all relationships are supportive. Recent research has found that *what happens* to women in relationships, as opposed to them simply having relationships, is the key. Unhealthy relationships actually *contribute* to women's increased risk for disappointment and depression. It is the quality of the relationship that makes the difference.

What kind of relationships provide a context for healing? Look for those that include the following factors.

The relationship should be with another woman who is on the same journey. A friend who is ignoring her own losses and still clinging tightly to her own dreams will not be a helpful sojourner on your quest for the truth. Your search will be a threat to her own determination to avoid the truth.

"I was talking to a friend who was struggling like I was," Carole said, "and before I knew it, I blurted out my anger about Rich's illness. My friend smiled sweetly and advised me to cheer up and count my blessings."

You may be fortunate enough to have a friend who is the perfect sojourner. If not, you may want to do what Carole finally did. "I joined a support group for caregivers. We share problems and solutions. We cry together, and we laugh about things no one else would understand. And not once has a person there told me to cheer up and count my blessings."

Look for a group that has as its focus the handling of disappointments or the understanding of childhood issues. If there are no such groups available, consider starting one yourself. You don't necessarily need special training to facilitate a group, especially if you use as your reference point a book such as this one, or *Steps to a New Beginning*, by Dr. Frank Minirth and other doctors of the Minirth-Meier Clinic. You can have each person work through the steps individually, and then discuss them together when you meet.

Understand that a supportive friend will neither minimize nor maximize your experience. Carole tended to minimize her disappointment. Again and again she would say, "It will work out all right. I mean, things could be a lot worse."

Minimizing can cause us to shut down emotionally, while maximizing will enlarge our disappointments. Sometimes we talk things over with a friend and she unconsciously fans the flames of our hurt by overreacting, almost as if the injury was done to her. One of the tasks of supportive friends is to help us maintain our objectivity. They cannot do that unless they first maintain their *own* objectivity.

Know that a healthy, supportive relationship is one characterized by mutuality. There should be give and take within your relationship. Sometimes the focus is on you; other times it is on your friend. A friend whose conversation only focuses on herself, or only focuses on you, cannot give supportive help. You need someone who can bring enough of herself to the relationship to let you know she is there, but not so much that she doesn't let you be there as well.

Vulnerability should grow between yourself and your supportive friend. "I meet with my supportive friend, and I talk about the weather, about books we've read, about the news—anything but my personal problems," Carole said. "It's not that I don't want her to know about Rich's condition, it's just that I'm afraid something will somehow reflect badly on me."

Vulnerability always carries with it some degree of risk. That's why it's important that your supportive friend be someone you can trust, someone you have known long enough for the security between you to grow and flourish.

Still, because none of us is 100 percent trustworthy, it may happen that your trust will be broken. But consider this: Some of the most solid relationships the two of us have encountered came only after someone had broken a trust, and both sides were willing to work through the hurt and misunderstandings it caused. Should one of your supportive friends break trust with you, spend some time seeing if that trust can be restored. If it can, your friendship will be deeper than ever.

Confidentiality is a part of trust.   "I told my friend about the problems I was having with my husband, and she shared the details with a prayer group," a woman told us. "By the time it got back to me, it sounded like we were getting a divorce! Now I feel worse than ever."

If you are going to meet with a group, or even if you are going to talk with just one or two people, it is vital that what you say be kept confidential. Here is a good principle for members of a support group to keep in mind: The only person who has the right to pass on confidential information is the one who shared it in the first place. No one else has that right unless she has been given specific permission.

Once we have begun building an effective support system around us, we are ready to move on to the next step: talking with our supportive friends or group about disappointments from our past. It is important that we share information with them, because we need their objectivity. We also want them to help keep us from getting lost in an intense archaeological search through our past—all we need to gather is enough information and examples to support our understanding of our present frustrations and needs.

The danger at this point is that we want to jump right into a mode of getting things resolved. But we need to take our time. Important emotional work needs to be done before we are ready to actually resolve these issues.

Once you understand the truth about your disappointments, you will be ready for the next critical part of healing—understanding and processing your emotional responses to those hurts and losses. This, basically, is a process of grieving.

2. Grieve Over Your Hurts and Losses

"When my husband went in for a checkup for some vague complaints, we got the shock of a lifetime," said Janelle. "The doctor told us he had cancer. Three months later he was dead." Within a few months of her husband's death, Janelle began seeing more and more of Ed. "I had known him casually for several years. Our sons were on the same Little League team. Ed was lonesome—his wife had left him five years earlier, so he was anxious to keep me company." Janelle and Ed married within the year. Five years later, they were divorced. "I never grieved my first husband's death," Janelle told us. "I don't think I have grieved the failure of my second marriage, either."

When we think of grieving, we usually think of it in terms of death, probably because the stages of grief were first identified when Dr. Elisabeth Kubler-Ross examined what we experience when someone close to us dies. But over the years, researchers and professionals have learned that this grieving process applies much further; it relates to *any* important loss. Although grieving is an essential step to healing, we often tend to overlook it as we attempt to deal with our disappointments.

We have to be able to experience our emotional responses in order to grieve; our ability to feel and express sadness in the face of loss or disappointment is a mark of our mental health. It is also an effective way to prevent more severe emotional problems from cropping up.

Sharing these emotional responses with our supportive friends seems to be especially important. But it's not enough just to feel things simply for the sake of feeling better. We have to be able to actually identify the emotions we have experienced in relation to our disappointments.

Determine Your Feelings Do you know what you are feeling? When we asked Carole, she said, "Sad, I guess. How else would I feel? I mean, my disappointments are no one's fault. I'm just sad."

Perhaps. But, like Carole, it might be helpful if you were to take some time to dig a little deeper for important clues from your past about how you are feeling today. Here are some ideas to help you bring back those buried feelings.

Use Old Photographs. Dig out old photographs of yourself as a child, the more pictures, the better. First arrange them in chronological order, then slowly and carefully sort through them. As you look at each picture, notice the expression on your face. Look at how you are dressed. Notice the details in the picture—your eyes, other people's expressions, the location, and so forth. Try to recall as much as you possibly can about the events that were taking place around the time of each photograph.

The photograph that especially caught Carole's eye was one that had been taken for the church directory when she was nine years old. "My whole family stood together, faces scrubbed, hair curled and combed, crisp fancy dresses or pressed suits and bow ties. We all had ear-to-ear grins on our faces. I remember that day. My mom and dad had a yelling argument on the way to the church, and when my brother begged them to stop, my mom slapped him across the face. My sister and I cried the whole way. But when we got to church, we wiped our eyes and smiled for the picture."

As you consider each photograph, ask God to reveal to you things you need to remember about that time of your life. Make notes of things that come to your mind, especially your feelings. ("Fear that our secret would be found out," Carole said.) Do any emotions well up within you as you look at photographs of a particular period? ("An overwhelming sense of shame and guilt.") If so, make notes about anything you can remember about that time. ("Duplicity was our way of life.")

Here are some other questions to consider as you work through your photos:

- Whom do you miss the most?
- Whom do you feel especially drawn toward? Why?
- Whom do you want to avoid as you look at these pictures?
- Who hurt you or others in your family?
- Who were the unloved people in your family?
- Who gave you the most? The least?
- What period of time seems absent or silent?

As you let the experience settle within you, continue to make notes of your feelings, memories, and questions. You may want to talk with family members about their memories of periods of time that concern you.

Were you frustrated by not being able to tell what you were feeling? Here is another way to help you access old, buried feelings.

Reflect Your Emotions in Art. You might find it helpful to draw pictures of the experiences you do remember. Some people draw these as a child might.

Other helpful art projects include sorting through old magazines and cutting out words and pictures that impress you, and then arranging them in a collage on a large piece of paper. When Erica did this, she was amazed to find that in all the pictures she cut out, there was not one single man. "I knew my father was absent a lot, but I never realized that in my mind he was nonexistent." Some people write poetry or short fictional stories that reflect some of their childhood experiences.

Whatever exercise you choose, approach it prayerfully.

Trust God to direct you to what is important for you to remember and to lead you to the place where you can identify and reexperience the feelings that were unacceptable to you as a child.

After you have spent some time reflecting on your photographs and drawings, write down what you felt. Include whatever feelings you think a person in that particular situation probably would have felt. If this is still difficult, imagine that a child living next door to you, someone you know and care about, is experiencing the same hurts you have just described. What might that little one be feeling? Does she feel angry? Is she afraid? Does she feel guilty? Especially consider the emotions of anger, fear, and guilt.

Anger is a natural response to the awareness that important people in our lives failed to meet real needs within us. "When I realized that my family was very detached from each other emotionally, it really made me mad!" said Sarah, the woman who so longs for emotional closeness with her husband. "I was so hungry inside. But neither my mother nor my father had time to be close to me—or maybe they weren't able to be. I was surprised at how angry it made me."

Mixed in with the feelings of anger will be feelings of fear. Often when we look at the stages of our childhood, we enter them as the child we were. When Sarah remembered a birthday party she missed when she was six years old, she emotionally reexperienced it as if she were still six years old. She felt fear in relation to the adults in that memory, "like I was all alone, totally unimportant."

In the same way, Sarah described guilt feelings. As a child of six, she still had some of the omnipotence of younger years, where she felt that whatever happened, or didn't happen, in her life was a direct consequence of her own behavior: "I remember myself as a bad little girl." Why else would Mom and Dad have been too preoccupied to notice her needs? Back then she blamed herself for her unmet need, just as she later blamed herself as an adult for the problems in her marriage.

Now that you've identified your hurts and the feelings attached to them, you are ready to grieve your losses.

3. Walk Through the Grieving Process

Elisabeth Kubler-Ross identified five stages in the grieving process. While we don't go through these stages in lockstep, we do tend to experience and reexperience them in some order. The first stage that Kubler-Ross identifies is *denial*. In the cycle of disappointment, denial is what keeps us holding on to our frustrating dreams, going back again and again until we finally give up and hit the wall of depression. In working through the steps in this chapter, we have been working on breaking out of our denial and facing the truth.

When we succeed, we hit the second stage: *anger*. In this chapter we will take a final look at our anger. The third stage is *bargaining* or *guilt*, and the fourth stage—where we turn the anger onto ourselves—is *depression*. The fifth stage, which we will look at later, is *acceptance*.

As we begin to experience our anger, we will at first blame everyone else for our impending death or for the death of a loved one. In the case of our disappointments, we blame others for what we can't have. Either way, we tend to think only in terms of the person we perceive as blocking our dream today. That's why Sarah blamed her husband for the lack of emotional closeness in their marriage and in her life, and Carole blamed Rich for not letting her talk about his disease and get the support she needed. But when Sarah and Carole focused their anger only on their husbands, it was an unhealthy expression of anger because it overlooked the roots of their disappointments. Only as they worked through the early steps could they begin to identify the other significant people in their past who also made them angry.

Some people think anger is the goal of grieving, but it is more like the doorway that leads us into sadness. To only stay angry is to remain in the process. It is unfinished. But never getting angry also keeps us stuck in an unfinished task. The goal of anger is to experience the sadness.

As Sarah worked on directing her anger toward its source, she found herself vacillating back and forth between the bargaining stage and the depression stage. "On the one hand, I had to set up conditions before I could forgive anyone or accept anything. But then I switched into blaming myself for my disappointments and I felt terrible." At other times she found herself wanting to deny the need for the whole process. This moved her right back into the first stage of the grief process. Compared to Carole who was grieving over her husband's impending death, Sarah's grieving could be described like this:

Stages	In Facing Death	In Disappointment
Denial	I won't die.	I won't admit I'm disappointed.
Anger	I blame others for letting death hurt me.	I blame others for my disappointment.
Bargaining	I set conditions that must first be fulfilled.	I set up conditions before I will accept my situation.
Depression	I blame myself for letting death hurt me.	I blame myself for my disappointment.

| Acceptance | I face my death with confidence. | I face my disappointment knowing I will grow through it. |

When we are angry in an unhealthy way, we channel our anger in only one direction—either at someone else for blocking our dreams or at ourselves for being unable to make those dreams come true. Healthy anger, on the other hand, is aimed in both directions. While we want to understand what has been broken inside us by others and to direct our anger at them, we also want to understand ourselves and the consequences of our brokenness. Unhealthy anger is focused on such things as our weaknesses, our inability to make things happen, or our stupidity or foolishness. Healthy anger focuses more on what we have lost and how that loss has limited us.

Here is an easy way to differentiate between healthy anger and unhealthy anger: When I have lost my keys somewhere in the house and I berate myself for being so stupid, I am demonstrating unhealthy anger. But if I can be angry and know that not being able to find my keys is not a moral failure on my part, I am showing healthy anger.

When Sarah expressed the sadness and emptiness she felt, she was demonstrating healthy anger toward herself. When she recognized that her parents had not only been emotionally distant to her, but had failed to teach her these important elements about relationships, her anger was also healthy. She was angry with them, but she was also angry at herself for having to live this way.

4. Share Your Sadness and Grief

There is a funny thing about grieving; it can never be done alone. If it is to be worked through to the stage of acceptance, the grieving process must be shared. But where our disappointments are concerned, the grief is not to be shared with those who have disappointed us early in our lives. To confront our parents with our hurts and our unmet needs would most likely only add to our injuries.

"I told my parents how their emotional coldness and distance had prevented me from having a satisfactory relationship with another adult, and they said I was crazy," Rosemary told us.

"When I confronted my father about the abuse I suffered at his hands over the years, he told me he was disciplining me the best way he knew how," Deborah said.

Women who have tried to confront their parents at this stage either find that, like Rosemary, their feelings and perceptions are dismissed as meaningless, or, like Deborah, they are argued out of their position. It's not that we are trying to protect our parents. We are simply recognizing that they still hold a powerful position in our lives. If there is to be any sharing with them, it comes much later in the process. Even then, it is optional.

By sharing your grieving process with your supportive friends, you will be "confessing" the sins that were done to you. In the Bible, the word *confession* means "to verbally agree with." Webster defines it this way: "To own or admit as true." In the Lord's Prayer, Jesus tells us we are to ask, "Forgive us our sins, as we forgive those who sin against us." In Nehemiah 9:2, the Israelites are called by the prophet Nehemiah to a celebration of the rebuilding of the walls around Jerusalem. As they begin that celebration, the Bible says, "They stood and confessed their sins and the iniquities of their fathers."

When we confess to the supportive people in our lives, we put anger in its proper perspective. We work through our feelings of guilt and arrive at a proper understanding of our own role in the events described. We emerge able to face our fears and see that they are not the monsters we believed them to be when we were still in denial.

PREVENTING A FUTURE FALL

When we get to this part of the process, we are finally able to give ourselves permission to ask the questions we weren't allowed to ask as children (perhaps we weren't even allowed to think them!). Now is the time and place for those "why" questions.

Here are some of Sarah's questions:

- "Why couldn't my parents care?"
- "Why couldn't they see I needed more from them?"
- "Why was our family so unfeeling? Didn't anyone else notice?"
- "Couldn't anyone tell I had deep feelings during that specific situation?"
- "Why doesn't anyone else in our family want closeness?"

No longer was Sarah the powerless child who had to keep her questions inside. Finally, at long last, she could ask them all. (Understand that these questions were not literally directed at family members. Sarah was asking them of herself and expressing them to her supportive friends.)

There are no answers to questions like these. But, then, we are not asking for answers. Simply asking gives us a sense of empowerment. We are just putting into words what we have been afraid to express for years. We are walking down a new street, one without a deep hole.

Personal Reflections:
Walking Through Your Grief

1. *Have you established a support system?*

_____

Write the names of those you consider to be your
supportive friends.

_____

_____

_____

_____

_____

2. *What have you discovered about your hurts and*
the feelings attached to them?

_____

_____

_____

_____

3. *Circle the word that describes the stage of grief*
with which you best identify.

DENIAL
ANGER
BARGAINING OR GUILT
DEPRESSION
ACCEPTANCE

Describe this stage in relation to your own disappointment.

_____

_____

_____

_____

_____

4. Think about sharing your disappointments. With whom are you going to share?

_____

What are you going to share with that person?

_____

_____

_____

When will you begin?

_____

Having grieved your losses, you are well on the road to recovery. Now it is time to forgive.

—10—

Canceling the Debts

J ust drive," Jan said angrily to Dave as she slammed the car door.

"Where do you want to go?" Dave asked.

"I don't care. Just go. Maybe to the beach or something."

"Do you want to talk about it?" he asked cautiously.

Silence from Jan.

"You know, it would help to talk about it," Dave said a bit more firmly.

Silence.

"There is nothing we can do. You know that."

Silence.

"It's done. It's over. Let's talk about something else."

"I don't understand you," Jan said. "Why aren't you angry, too? They took advantage of us! They ripped us off, then turned it around so it seemed to be our fault. I just don't understand you!"

We had just endured a long and terribly frustrating court battle. "I had lived most of my life under the assumption that people who stayed away from trouble and out of people's way, never accusing or offending, didn't get slapped with lawsuits," Jan said. "But it didn't happen that way for us."

The people who bought our house seemed so nice. Sure, they were making a lot of demands, but aren't people often uptight when they are taking such a big step? When they signed the contract saying they would pay the loan on the house, they were making us a promise. And the bank agreed that they were trustworthy to pay.

Three months later, we heard from the bank. Not a single payment had been made, and the bank claimed we were still responsible for that loan! When we called the new residents, they said, "Oh, we fully intend to pay. We'll catch up."

That was just the beginning of a long battle. What had started out as a favor to someone else ended up being financially devastating to us.

"It's over," Dave said calmly. "Let it go."

"But the judge didn't even want to hear our side!" Jan protested. "How can you just accept this? It's so unfair!"

Jan knew the principles of working through disappointments, but right then she couldn't use one of them. She couldn't pray. She couldn't talk about the problem. And she didn't feel a bit like forgiving.

Forgive and let go. These are vital steps toward recovery. It is true whether the debt is relatively small, or one that is crushingly huge.

One of the reasons we tend to avoid looking back at the issues in our past is that we feel so helpless to do anything about them. "Let the past stay in the past," people often say. What they don't realize is that anything not resolved in our past is always seeking to find some way to express itself in our present. Only when past issues are resolved do we become free of their intrusion into our daily lives.

Throughout most of her childhood, Deborah was sexually abused by her father, a minister. "On my tenth birthday, after my candles were blown out and the cake and ice cream were gone, I told my mother what he was doing," she said. "Mom told me Daddy wouldn't do anything to hurt me and not to bring it up again. When my sister told me he was after her, too, I finally confronted him. My father pulled out his Bible, pointed out a couple of verses, and said it was his job to love me and my job to obey him. I was wrong and he was right. That's how it's always been in our house."

The tension of wanting to *do* something drives us to confront those who have failed to meet our childhood needs. "Last week, for the first time since I was fourteen, I confronted my father," Deborah continued. "I told him he had ruined my life, and that at the very least he owed me an apology. He basically told me I was one messed up lady and it was all my fault."

Confrontation is just another form of trying harder. The real tension is within yourself: Is there anything you can do to resolve the issue, or are you stuck with just standing still and being understanding?

Compare this predicament to that of a person who is afraid of water. After struggling to understand why she is afraid, she finally comes to an awareness of some trauma earlier in her life that so frightened her about water that even crossing a bridge makes her anxious. But now that she understands *why* she is nervous, crossing a bridge is even more traumatic than before.

Understanding our fear will never, by itself, resolve that fear. Resolving what we now understand about our disappointments requires that we take action.

When Deborah was told that taking action would involve forgiving her father, she protested. "I could never do that! How could I condone what he did to me?" This was the same question Jan was asking Dave.

Like many of us, Deborah has a distorted view of what forgiveness means. Before you protest at the idea of forgiving the person who caused your disappointments, read on about some of the myths we have attached to forgiveness, and what forgiveness is really all about.

WHAT FORGIVENESS IS *NOT*

"We went out of our way to be more than fair with them and they took advantage of us," Jan said. "They just cannot be trusted!"

"How can anyone expect me to be reconciled with my father or my mother?" Deborah asked. "Neither one has done a thing to deserve it! We will never really be a family again."

Forgiveness Is Not Reconciliation.

Forgiveness is a unilateral process—that is, it's something we do *without* the involvement of the person being forgiven. If we had to be involved with that person, what would happen if he, like Deborah's father, was still in denial about his behavior? Or what if that person has died? Then we're stuck. We can never forgive. That leaves that other person in control of the forgiving process. No, it doesn't work that way.

You can forgive the person who failed you without ever even talking with that person about it. You only need to talk about it with your supportive friends so you can work through the process with someone you trust. The person who failed you is not part of that process. Later, when you are finished with the forgiving process, you may want to talk with that person, but that's totally up to you. It is in no way a necessary part of forgiving.

Reconciliation, on the other hand, is a bilateral process. It *does* involve the other person. True reconciliation can only take place when that other person is in a vulnerable, truth-seeking process of her own. If, after Deborah finishes processing her disappointments and her early unmet needs, she wants to talk with her parents about what she has learned about herself and her family, she might test the water with a small, safe piece of information. She could see if they were interested in understanding the truth, or whether they wanted to remain in denial and continue to ignore the truth as she had experienced it.

For example, Deborah might share her feelings of abandonment and distrust with her mother. She might ask her, "Do you remember struggling with wanting our family to feel closer to each other?" or "Did you ever wish you could talk openly with Grandma?" Whether she goes any further depends on how her mom responds.

Reconciliation can only take place in a safe environment.

Forgiveness Is Not Condoning or Excusing.

In his book *Forgive and Forget*, Lewis Smedes writes: "Excusing is just the opposite of forgiving. We excuse people when we understand that they were not to blame. . . . We forgive people for things we blame them for."

Never make light of what you have identified as a painful part of your past. You have been on a search for truth, and your purpose has not been to deny it once again by saying it was all okay, that it didn't really matter.

In true forgiveness, there is always an awareness of the anger you felt—and may still feel—at the offense that took place. Smedes asks, "Is there anger after forgiving?" His answer: "Yes, often. It can't be helped. Some people believe that they should not feel anger in their hearts once they forgive. I do not agree." He goes on to point out that anger and forgiveness can operate within a person at the same time. Anger does not mean you have failed at forgiving. The point is to work through that anger and to come to the place where you can release it. This is never done by saying something is okay that is not okay![1]

Forgiveness Is Not Always Done Quickly.

Deborah has begun to work through the hurt and anger she feels toward her parents, but it will take her a long time. She says she isn't ready to try and see them or to talk to them about her feelings. Although she is still in the forgiving process, she is moving in the right direction. It is all right for her to take whatever time she needs. Because the offense against her was great, and because it happened early in her development, it will take a long time for her to process her feelings and come to the place where she can let go and forgive.

WHAT FORGIVENESS *IS*

So what is forgiveness? We can define it in two ways: One is "Fixing something in me that someone else broke." We take responsibility to work on the problem ourselves rather than to keep hoping that the person to blame will come along and fix things. True personal freedom comes only when we are able to take responsibility for what needs to happen in our lives. Forgiveness gives us that freedom. It is something we do for our own good.

The other definition of forgiveness comes from the Apostle Paul. He tells us that forgiveness is the canceling of a debt (Col. 2:13–14). When we forgive the offending person or persons, we are recognizing that they can never repay the debt they owe us. Therefore, for our own sake, we are canceling the debt.

When a bank forgives a loan, it isn't done for the sake of

the borrower. And it certainly isn't done because the borrower has been such a good customer and has earned the respect of the bank. No, it is done when the borrower has absolutely no way to repay the debt. It is done in the bank's best interest, so the loan can be written off and the bank can get on with its business. In the same way, we forgive so that we can write off the uncollectible debt owed to us and get on with our lives.

Dr. Smedes points out that, "When you forgive someone for hurting you, you perform spiritual surgery inside your soul; you cut away the wrong that was done to you so that you can see your 'enemy through the magic eyes' that can heal your soul. Detach that person from the hurt and let it go, the way a child opens his hands and lets a trapped butterfly go free."

When we open our hands, we are saying goodbye to our expectations that the person who disappointed us will ever be able to repay the debt.

SAYING GOODBYE TO UNMET EXPECTATIONS

We can benefit from creating a ritual, or a symbol, that helps us say goodbye to our expectations about the person we are forgiving. Sarah decided she would have a funeral ceremony for the emotionally distant parents she had. She found a shoe box and placed her journal inside it. She also tucked in a picture of her parents. Then she invited her supportive friends over and placed the shoe box in the fireplace. She had written out a "funeral service" for her parents, and she and her friends went through the service together. When they finished, they lit the fireplace and watched the flames devour the box and all that was inside.

"I wasn't symbolically killing my parents, or cutting them out of my life," Sarah said. "What I was destroying was the image of them I had created in my mind and had expected them to live up to. When I realized they could never be the parents I wished for—and even if they could be now, I was no longer the child who needed it—I decided I would bury my image of what I expected from them. That's what burned in my fireplace."

Was that the end of Sarah's struggle with her expectation? "No," she said. "So I decided to go out to a cemetery nearby on a windy day when no one could hear, and have a conversation with my 'dead' parents. I yelled at them. I vented all the emotions I had identified within me. I've done it twice now, and I think I'm finally finished."

"How are you relating to your parents now?" we asked her.

"I feel different," Sarah told us. "They haven't changed, but my expectations of them have. I think I'm finally able to see them as they really are, with all their limitations."

For the first time, Sarah felt free to decide who she was and what she really wanted in her life. "For me, the forgiving was the releasing of my expectations," she added. "And I'm the one who benefited from that step."

CANCELING THE FAMILY DEBT

Along with your ritual, it is important that you take time to pray about the release you want to experience, not only from the debt you feel people owe you, but also from the debts that may have been carried within your family for generations. Giving and receiving forgiveness for destructive family patterns will bring a balanced perspective that may help you understand the reality of your experience.

Personal Reflections:
Forgiving

1. When you think of forgiveness as the canceling of a debt that cannot be paid, what are some of the debts you have a hard time releasing?

Debt	Person Involved

2. Where are you today in the forgiving process?

_____

_____

_____

_____

_____

_____

3. Are you experiencing some fears and apprehensions about forgiving the person who has caused your disappointments?

_____

_____

What are they?

_____

_____

_____

_____

_____

4. *In what ways do these fears and apprehensions suggest that you are still in the process of forgiving and not yet at the point where you can cancel the debt?*

_____

_____

_____

_____

_____

5. *Periodically, think over the debts you listed above. As you are able to forgive each one, draw a line through that debt and write CANCELED across it. (You will probably not be able cross them all out immediately. Some debts will be easier to forgive than others. Allow yourself as much time as you need.)*

Note: If you are finding it really difficult to forgive a particular debt, set a time in the future when you will sit down again and work toward canceling that debt. Make the time specific and mark it on your calendar.

Now that we have worked through the past, what do we do with the present and the future? Can we possibly dare to dream again? If so, is there any chance those dreams could actually become reality? In the next chapter, we will discover a process that will help us find the courage to dream again, and even more, to find fulfillment for our dreams.

— 11 —

Finding the Courage to Dream Again

Ⅰn this chapter we will look at our dreams and adjust them to reality. Then we will look at how we can dream new dreams in the future. This process is as new as the twentieth century and as old as 1100 B.C., when a godly woman named Hannah lived in ancient Israel. We can adjust our old dreams to reality by following Hannah's example.

HANNAH FOUND COURAGE TO LOOK AT HER DREAMS REALISTICALLY

The High Holy Days of Judaism take place in the late fall of each year. Sometimes called the "days of Awe," the ten days of Rosh Hashanah mark the beginning of the new year in the Jewish calendar. On the first day of Rosh Hashanah, Jews gather together to chant the *Haftarah*, the portion of scripture that tells the story of Hannah, for it is a story closely tied to one of the basic themes of Rosh Hashanah: "God remembers."

Although the account of Hannah as recorded in 1 Samuel

1:1–2:10 is brief and sketchy, it doesn't take much imagination to fill in some of the gaps in the story and to identify with Hannah's hurts. Her disappointments built year after year after year, until finally the pain was more than she could bear.

Hannah, married to a man who had two wives, lived in a culture where a wife's value in the eyes of her husband depended upon her ability to have children, especially sons. Peninnah, the other wife, had given birth to both sons and daughters, but Hannah was childless. According to the customs of the day, Peninnah should have been her husband's favorite and Hannah should have been ignored. But Hannah was the favored one. Elkanah loved her deeply and generously gave her anything she needed. You can imagine how Peninnah felt. Filled with resentment toward Hannah, Peninnah taunted her constantly about her inability to have children. Peninnah made Hannah's life miserable.

Hannah's disappointment at having no child of her own, already great, was multiplied by Peninnah's jeering and the humiliation Hannah felt for letting her husband down. So Hannah did what many of us do: She turned to God for help. But year after year after year passed, and nothing changed.

Elkanah could not understand why Hannah was so devastated by this disappointment. "Am I not better to you than ten sons?" he asked her.

In considering the responses we got to our survey, Elkanah's question was not unreasonable. Many women said they could bear just about anything if their husbands would genuinely stand beside them. One woman spoke for many when she said, "If it was him and me against the world, I would be satisfied." Yet, for Hannah, her husband's openness and affection were not enough. She pushed him away and couldn't accept his love, for she was convinced, "He has to be as disappointed in me as I am in myself."

Isn't that a lot like us? Some really good and important parts of our dreams may have been fulfilled, yet because of our need for one essential part, something that is still lacking, we languish in pain and tears.

During the family's yearly trip to Shiloh to worship the Lord, during their meal one evening, Peninnah provoked and teased Hannah until she wept bitterly. When that miserable dinner was finally over, Hannah went to the temple to pray.

Now, Hannah's was not just an everyday prayer. The Bible tells us she "was in bitterness of soul, and prayed to the Lord and wept in anguish." We don't know what she prayed, but it's easy to imagine: "Would it be so hard to give me just *one* son?" Oh, the pain and sadness that must have been poured out in that prayer! Oh, the envy that consumed her when she looked at Peninnah's children. She must have lashed out at the injustice of it all.

Even though Hannah's prayer was silent, her anguish was so evident that Eli, the priest, who was watching, was certain she was drunk. When he reprimanded her, she assured him, "I have not had so much as a drop of wine to drink." Then she poured out the hurt that flooded her soul.

HANNAH "GAVE BACK" HER DREAM

In the midst of your disappointments, have you ever tried to make a deal with God? We certainly have. "God, if you will give me what I ask, I will. . . ."

Hannah didn't bargain with God. She didn't say, "God, if You will give me a son, I'll be the best wife and mother in all of Israel." No, what Hannah did was make a vow to God: "If You will give me a son, I will give him to the Lord all the days of his life."

Sounds paradoxical, doesn't it? "If You give me what I want, I will give it back to You." Something had changed in

Hannah's heart. She was giving up what she so desperately desired even before she had it. And God responded by giving her what she wanted.

Hannah did not break her vow. When her son, Samuel, was born, Hannah kept him until he was weaned, then she took him to Shiloh and left him there with Eli. And so she was separated from the son she had longed for so desperately.

And so it is with us. We must come to the place where we are willing to let go of what we so desperately desire, for often in the letting go, we can finally begin to dream again.

"But how can I let go when my expectation is that my husband will be emotionally available to me?" you might be saying. Or "How can I let go of my expectation that my wayward child will turn out okay?" Carole asked us. "How can I let go of my dream that my husband will again be like he was? I picture him back at work. I imagine him helping our son restore his MG. I see him walking straight and tall, reading the newspaper, paying the bills. I imagine him having a real, caring conversation with me, and holding me and loving me like he used to do. How can I let go of all that?"

How do we let go when we have done everything right, yet everything still is turning out so bad? Certainly we must wrestle with such questions before we can even dare to hope again. Let's begin by reviewing the healing process in terms of Hannah's experience.

HANNAH LET GO OF THE PAST

Actually, Hannah acted like many of us. Carole, too, clung persistently to her dream that, in spite of the evidence, Rich's illness would just go away. Like Hannah, in order to hold on, Carole had to either deny her pain or to repress it, and this just heaped disappointment on top of disappointment.

But before Hannah's last anguished trip to the tabernacle, an important change took place. She stopped demanding that God fit into her plans and heal her disappointment *her* way. This change made such a profound difference in her life that Hannah went to Shiloh a different woman.

As the story progresses, Hannah's dream also changes. Before Shiloh, she may have dreamed of having her own child so she could show off to Peninnah, or at least so she could shut her up. She may have dreamed of both her and her husband's enjoyment as they played with the little one. But in making her vow with the Lord, she gave up a large part of her dream.

When Eli told her, "Go in peace, and the God of Israel grant your petition which you have asked of Him," Hannah believed him. She not only let go of certain aspects of her dream about the child, she also let go of the struggle to make the dream come true. She heard the words of the priest, and she accepted them as fact. Now, that's faith.

As we begin to mend our dreams, we, too, need to move over into the arena of faith. Our solution just may not be God's solution. Saying goodbye to our disappointment means releasing our solution and, by faith, opening our hands to receive God's solution.

But that's not all. Hannah also found her fulfillment somewhere else.

GOD'S PLAN FOR FULFILLMENT

When we look up the opposite of the word *disappointment,* we find the word *fulfillment.* "Fulfillment has to be one of life's choicest gifts," says Charles Swindoll. "A major building block toward authentic happiness. Solomon must have had it in mind when he wrote in Proverbs 13:19, 'Desire realized is sweet to the soul. . . .'" (NASV).

Once we have broken our cycle of disappointment, we can walk a new path toward fulfillment. For Hannah, fulfillment came from obedience to the Lord and the knowledge that He truly had remembered her, not from having her own children around her. Many of us will also find our fulfillment in a totally different place than where we had expected it to be. Be willing to look beyond your own narrow limits and ask God to show you the fulfillment He has for you.

One woman said that a very important dream in her life was to become a teacher. "All my life I have enjoyed children, and I thought the best way to be around them was to teach in elementary school," she said.

When her college career was repeatedly interrupted, her disappointment grew as her goal of teaching seemed to fade away. "But then I realized that the *real* need behind my desire to teach was to be with children, and I am finding all kinds of ways to be involved with them." Yes, she did finish her degree. "But I don't feel such an urgent need to teach anymore. Who knows? I may do something totally different, but whatever it is, I know it will involve me with children."

As we seek other ways to fulfill the need that is the root of our disappointment, we will often struggle with tension between building healthy dreams for our future and falling back into the old patterns of behavior that led to our disappointment in the first place. Obviously, life is still going to have its disappointing experiences. We can never totally say goodbye to disappointment. But we can say goodbye to the destructive pattern of dealing with our disappointments in the same old way. And we can move into the future with dreams, goals, and expectations that are based on the truths about ourselves and those around us. We can learn to dream again! But this time our dreams will be touched by reality.

The secret for you lies in how you hold on to your dreams

about the future and in how you perceive your life as it exists right now. It's important to come to the place where you can see yourself, and others in your life, more accurately. When your viewpoint about life is rooted in an accurate understanding, you can experience dreams and hopes that can come true.

Do you want to dream new dreams that can come true? Here are nine important guidelines that will help you do just that.

PAUL LEARNED HOW TO DREAM NEW DREAMS

The Apostle Paul experienced many disappointments. He set out to convert the people around the Mediterranean, yet all too often he was run out of town or shipwrecked or almost killed (Imagine yourself hiding from your enemies in a basket and being lowered from the top of the enormous town walls so you can escape!). As he tried to dream new, realistic dreams, he developed principles that we can also use to learn to dream again in spite of the circumstances.

1. Be Honest About Yourself and Others.

When Paul wrote to the church at Rome, he urged them to "be honest in your estimate of yourselves" (Rom. 12:3 TLB). This is where every one of us must begin. It's a difficult thing to do. We usually err on both sides: We think too little of ourselves when it comes to valuing who we are, and we think too much of ourselves when we consider what we can do in any given situation. So how do we arrive at the place where we can "think soberly" about ourselves?

"From the beginning, I was convinced I could make Rick fight against the ravages of Huntington's Disease," Carole said, "and if he would fight, then he would get better—or at least wouldn't get worse."

To think soberly requires that we recognize our own limitations and the limitations of those upon whom we are depending. In other words, we become honest about what we *can* do as well as what we *cannot* do. And we honestly face what the other person involved can and cannot do. In each case, it may not be a question of willingness, but of ability.

Many women, after reflecting on what they had written on their survey sheets, added something like this: "My husband probably doesn't even know how to be the kind of person I've wanted him to be all these years." This kind of honesty is painful, for it forces us to *see what is rather than what we wish it were.*

We will also find ourselves becoming more honest with God about our feelings. The respect many of us have been taught to have for authority figures spills over into the way we talk with God, but if we can't honestly pour out our hearts to God about everything inside us, whom can we talk to? He is the only one who truly knows every part of us and accepts us anyway.

How freeing it is to become comfortable talking to God this way! He is not threatened by our emotions, nor is He put off by our anger. He already knows what is in our hearts—He is just waiting for us to share it with Him.

2. Learn to Be Content.

One of Paul's most profound statements is in the letter he wrote near the end of his life while he was imprisoned in Rome. It was a time of great sadness and disappointment for him. Paul had planned to go to Rome as a free man and to continue on to Spain, but before he even started, he was arrested and put into chains. Yet in prison he wrote these incredible words, which we read so often and wish were true for us: "I have learned in whatever state I am, to be content." He continues, "I know how to be abased, and I know how to abound. Everywhere and in all things I have learned both to be full and to be hungry, both to abound and to suffer need" (Phil. 4:11–12).

We can only be content in the present when we have resolved the issues of the past. When Paul says, "One thing I do, forgetting those things which are behind and reaching forward to those things which are ahead" (Phil. 3:13), he is not using denial as the means of dealing with the past. He is recognizing that until the issues of our past are resolved, they will continue to express themselves in some way. No amount of denial will keep them buried. There has to be resolution. That resolution allowed Paul to be content within his circumstances.

Are you still struggling with contentment in your circumstances? Is the work still unfinished? If so, you may just need time to feel settled about them. Or perhaps God is pointing to something else that needs attention in your life. Ask Him to show you what it is.

3. *Speak the Truth in Love.*

This step is about confrontation—not confronting the people in your past, but learning how to confront the people in your life now. And it has nothing to do with an angry scene.

Let's look again at Paul and a letter he wrote from a different prison. In Ephesians 4:15 he says that we grow in Christ, partially through "speaking the truth in love." A little later on in the same chapter, he adds, "Putting away lying, 'Let each one of you speak truth with his neighbor'" (Eph. 4:25). Now, here, *lying* does not refer only to obvious dishonesty, but also to more subtle forms. Do you ever hedge the truth with your husband because you don't want to make him angry? Have you skirted around subjects with your mother because you didn't see any reason to "upset her"? Do you sometimes tell a caller that "the check is in the mail" because you don't want to discuss your financial struggles? Most of us have. Yet these forms of lying rob us of our integrity and of the contentment we seek.

Here is the pattern Paul gives us: We are to speak truth, but we are to speak it in love. Sound hard? Here are some guidelines on how to confront in love:

Speak in Love, Not in Anger. Usually we either speak in love or we speak the truth, but we have a hard time doing both at the same time. Yet that's exactly what we are to do.

Here is an example: A wife is always protecting her husband and letting him off the hook. If he fails to understand her emotional needs or concerns, she says something like, "Honey, I know you're tired. We don't have to talk about this now," or "I'm sorry, it was all my fault. I know I'm pressuring you, so let's just change the subject."

When you fall back into your old patterns like this, you will probably think you have blown the whole process. But understand that at any point in a conversation, you can correct your focus and "speak the truth with love." As soon as you become aware of what you are doing, stop and say something like, "No, that's not what I wanted to say. I'm not going to let this just go by—it's too important to me. I want you to not only hear what I am saying, but also to pay attention to what I am feeling."

The same is true when you err on the side of anger, although this is much harder to correct on the spot, since the other person's anger has probably also been triggered. Still, you can stop yourself and say something like, "I'm sorry I've gotten so angry. I'm afraid you'll only hear my anger and miss what is really important to me. Let's talk about this later when I've cooled down."

These examples are not suggestions of how to "say it

right." As we have seen, saying it right is no guarantee that it will come true. We are simply trying to show how important it is to stop those old patterns and bring our communication back into balance by speaking the truth with love. We need to act responsibly with ourselves and to express more clearly what we need from that other person. In doing this, we will also be allowing him or her to enjoy the privilege of being responsible as well.

Describe Exactly What You Need.   When you get caught up in a cycle of disappointment, do you tend to complain to everyone except the person directly involved? Sometimes we have been so hurt and have so neglected what we want and need that we don't know how to express it directly. Here is a technique that has helped other women: Choose three things that are of primary importance to you in a given situation and concentrate only on them.

Carole was disappointed in the responses of her family and her husband's family. "They didn't talk much about what was happening, they weren't there to listen to my frustrations and fears, and they weren't offering to help me carry the load that was wearing me out." We suggested that Carole make a list of all the things she wanted from the family, then that she go back over it and pick out the three most important things. Carole listed: (1) Don't criticize what I am doing unless you have suggestions to offer, (2) Be willing to talk to me and let me talk to you, (3) Offer to watch him now and then so I can get out of the house.

"What about all the other things on my list?" she asked us.

"Let them go," we told her.

Over the years, other people learn that if they can get us to talk about all the things that bother us, they are off the hook. Since they can't possibly do everything we expect, the important things get lost in the crowd. But if you focus on three important things, the message will gradually get through. Then it's up to the others to decide what they are going to do.

Don't Explain or Defend What You Need. "I tried to tell them why I needed time off," Carole said. "Time for a dentist appointment or grocery shopping was easy, but when I tried to explain why I wanted to go to lunch with friends or to a movie once in a while, I started to feel selfish and guilty."

Trying to explain why you want or need what you are asking for is another sure way to get off track. Because most of us have been trained to explain, it is very easy to fall into this trap. But the more we explain, the more reasons the other person will find for not doing anything.

As soon as you become aware that you are explaining, stop! You do not have to defend what you desire. If you don't explain, you may get what you want, or you may not. But if you do explain, you will be guaranteeing that you *won't* get it.

Repeat Your Request Until You Are Heard. "I asked my sister-in-law for a Thursday afternoon, then a Friday morning, then some time on Saturday," Carole said. "When none of those times would work for her, I said, 'I know you're busy, too, but I need some time off.' Then I asked *her* to set a time. We were finally able to work out a schedule of three hours every Tuesday."

The purpose of our old patterns of communicating our needs was to change either the other people involved, or to change the situations. Now, because we are emotionally letting go of what we held on to in our dreams, we simply desire to be heard. This is an important part of speaking the truth in love.

When we begin to be more direct in our communication, the others involved will often keep on responding to us as if we were still communicating in our old pattern. They will try to push our buttons and sidetrack the conversation, or to bring up old issues, or to ask for specifics—whatever worked in the past to get us off center. Now, with the pattern broken, they will probably step up these efforts. A simple way to sidestep the problem is to respond by saying, "I understand what you are saying, *but.* . . ." Then repeat what you said in the first place. You can keep on doing this over and over until the other person tells you he or she has finally heard you.

4. Become More Flexible.

The Apostle Paul was a driven man. Part of his greatness came from his tremendous drive to establish and stabilize churches in as many places as he could. At least two times, though, when all his plans were thrown aside, he found he needed to go in a different direction. One was when the Spirit told him to go to Macedonia, including Philippi; the other was when he went to Rome in chains instead of as a free man. His spirit of contentment meant he was not only driven, but he was also flexible.

In Romans 8:28, Paul writes, "We know that all things work together for good to those who love God." Perhaps you've read this promise and wondered how your husband's emotional coldness could possibly work for your good. Perhaps you have questioned how your child's rejection of you and everything you value could work together for good. "What about my husband?" Carole asked. "When he was healthy, he was serving God! How can his illness be for good?"

These are hard questions. In his letter to the Philippians, Paul writes from prison, "I want you to know, brethren, that the things which happened to me have actually turned out for the furtherance of the gospel" (Phil. 1:12). Imagine that! Here is Paul, the victim of a gross injustice, choosing to "swim with the current." In no way is he passive about what is happening, for he protests the injustice every time he gets the opportunity. The ability to actively swim with the current requires that we develop a sense of flexibility that will allow us to effectively handle whatever develops.

` In the second chapter of his letter, Paul urges us to "let this mind be in you, which was also in Christ Jesus." Then he points out how Jesus willingly "let go" of His status as God, and willingly "humbled Himself."

Is Paul suggesting we go back to quietly suffering the pain and hopelessness of our situations? Absolutely not! Never was Jesus a passive victim of His circumstances. Even when He was faced with the greatest injustice of all—death on the cross—He moved ahead with a purpose, making choices at every step. People who are victims believe they have no choices. People who know they have choices, whether they choose to act on them or not, are never victims.

All too often, when we are pushed to the wall, we can only think of our choices in terms of extremes. Remember Sarah, the woman whose childhood need for emotional closeness continued to affect her relationship with her husband? She said, "Over the years I've tried everything to reach my husband on an emotional level. Now I'm finally facing facts. I can either give in and accept my lot in life, or I can leave him."

Because our frustration and hurt have blinded us to the options available to us, we may need objective input from others to help us find our flexibility again.

Once Sarah has identified the unmet needs represented by her disappointment in her husband, she can find other ways to find fulfillment in her life. For example, she might develop abilities that can put her into a job that has a lot of meaningful people-to-people contact. Or she may find that there are things she can do in her church that will be meaningful to her. Or she can volunteer to do things that matter to her. In order to do this, Sarah will not only learn how to say "yes" to helpful situations, she will also need to learn to say "no" to those that don't fit her needs.

Sarah can develop friendships that are meaningful to her. Her husband may not like her friends, but in finding options, she is not going to limit her activities simply to fit his plans. In becoming more flexible, she may even say "no" to her husband's plans.

Any actions we take to bring flexibility into our lives must be done with a caring, loving attitude, never with a desire for revenge or with spiteful anger.

5. Examine Your Thoughts.

Which things are we responsible for and which are outside our responsibility? One way to differentiate between the two is to examine our thoughts. Paul tells us we are to be transformed by the renewing of our minds (Rom. 12:2). How? By "bringing every thought into captivity to the obedience of Christ," he writes (2 Cor. 10:5). This is the only way to monitor our thoughts. Bringing every thought into captivity means listening carefully to the things we are telling ourselves in the privacy of our own minds, especially when we are experiencing disappointments.

It may help to write out the kinds of things you are saying to yourself. Carole told us, "Whenever I become aware of the heaviness of my disappointments, I look back at the things I was thinking about just before, and jot them down in a small notebook I carry around in my purse." Over time, Carole was able to look back through her notes and identify some thought patterns that were related to her feelings of hopelessness and disappointment.

So often we simply let our minds go wherever they want

to go without ever realizing the impact our thoughts have on our emotions. Part of changing the way we feel means capturing our thoughts and seeing where they are taking us. As you monitor your thoughts, look for repetitive themes and beliefs that set you up for additional disappointments and frustrations. Here's what Carole found: "The thoughts that came up over and over again were that the troubles were somehow my fault."

Now examine the thoughts you have written and ask yourself such questions as these: How much do I really believe what I am telling myself? Is it accurate? Is it Biblical? Then take some time to share your thinking with your supportive friends. Ask them for feedback on how accurate your thoughts are. After that, check your thoughts against your feelings.

"My supportive friends all said the same thing: 'How could this possibly be your fault? Rick has a genetic condition!'" Carole told us. "When I checked my thoughts against my feelings, I came back again and again to the same conclusion—I was consumed with guilt for something that couldn't possibly be my fault!"

Do certain feelings typically follow the thought patterns you are experiencing? Challenge the thoughts you take for granted.

How about the things you are saying about yourself? If a friend said those things about you, would you be hurt or insulted? Then why are you telling such things to yourself? It's important that we be careful about the way we talk to ourselves, for eventually we will end up believing what we hear. Make certain that what you believe squares with what God thinks about you. (If you want a picture of how God thinks about you, read through Romans 5–8 in one sitting. Read it several times, focusing especially on what Paul says in chapter eight about God's unconditional acceptance and His endless love.)

6. *Search Out Alternatives.*

You've probably spent a lot of time thinking about what would happen if your dream were to actually come true. Now imagine what would happen if your dream *never* came true. What paths would be open to you that you could take?

"I can't do this," Carole told us, "because I don't have any options."

There are always options. Take time now to think of as many as you can. Don't evaluate any of the ideas that come into your mind. Concentrate on stirring up all the possible paths you can take to either change your life circumstances or to change your reactions and responses to the people who are the focus of your disappointment. Write down every alternative you can think of, then discuss the ramifications and consequences of each one with your supportive friends.

When we finally convinced Carole to try this exercise, she was amazed at how long her list was. "From that list has come an amazingly successful alternative," she told us. "Rich is working a couple of hours a day in a sheltered workshop with other handicapped people. He stays busy, he feels better about himself, he earns a little money, and I get a break each day."

You may be surprised at some of the new ideas you have overlooked!

7. *Anticipate the Good.*

As we live with disappointments year after year, we train ourselves to anticipate the hurt. If you are going to say goodbye to your disappointments, you are going to have to retrain yourself to see and anticipate the good. We aren't suggesting you set yourself up by thinking your dreams really will come true after all. We are simply saying you can begin to think that something nice just might be about to happen.

When Sarah worked through this step, she started noticing that her husband—in his own way—really was trying to
please her. "Sure, he is way short of what I had hoped he
would do," she said. "But because of my disappointment, I
hadn't even seen the things he *was* doing."

As Sarah started to anticipate good things in their relationship, she was more open to seeing the small things she
had missed before. "It didn't make everything wonderful,"
she told us, "but it did reduce the tension between us. And I
do think he tried even harder as a result of my noticing what
he was doing."

Sarah also noticed that she was feeling less internal tension. As she changed her focus, she started to relax. "I could
actually feel some of the heaviness in me lessen," she said.

This was a more difficult exercise for Carole, but she, too,
benefited. "It is so sad and depressing to see Rich deterio-
rate. What really helped me was when I started doing a
Bible study on heaven. It really helps to understand that
this life is just a transitory stage of our existence and that
the time will come when he and I will be reunited, healthy
and whole, to live forever in the presence of God."

8. Review Your Day.

Would you like to challenge and change some of the depressive patterns of your thinking? Then try this: At the end
of each day, take about ten minutes to review the events of
that day in terms of the changes that are taking place within
you. Consider some of the positive things that are happening and some of the good things you are experiencing.

This exercise is especially helpful if you actually write the
events down in a notebook. Carole records hers in a pink-
flowered journal she calls her blessing book. Over time, she
has accumulated a record of the good things in her life as
well as the growth she has been experiencing. "When I feel

discouraged and disappointed, I read through my blessing book," she says. "It gives me a more balanced perspective than I've ever before had in my life."

9. Move Toward Your Goal.

"I press toward the goal for the prize of the upward call of God in Christ Jesus," Paul writes in Philippians 3:14. He had a goal, and he was committed to reach it. Having a goal means deciding what is important to us. No longer will we live by someone else's agenda. With God's help, we will set the agendas for ourselves.

This is a tough step, for it requires that you take responsibility for yourself. It also means giving up responsibility for those things that are beyond your control. While these two actions are difficult in different ways, both can become excuses for not getting on with your own life.

The Serenity Prayer of Alcoholics Anonymous puts it this way: "God grant us serenity to accept the things we cannot change, courage to change the things we can, and wisdom to know the difference." Carole has a stained-glass lightcatcher with this prayer on the windowsill above her kitchen sink. Every time she is tempted to take responsibility for something beyond her control, she looks at the lightcatcher and prays the prayer.

Getting the responsibility question sorted out will free you to move forward. That can be exciting, but it can also be frightening. Often we get a weird type of comfort with that old disappointment pattern. And our tendency is to stay with the comfortable rather than launch into the new and untested future. But you have worked through the steps of the process, and you are ready to take on that responsibility.

"Imitate me, just as I also imitate Christ," Paul writes (1 Cor. 11:1). This imitation is an attitude, one that is willing

"To let go and let God" so He can fill your every need just as He promised He would. If you are willing to take the risk to test His promises, you will find that He really is a God who never disappoints.

LETTING GO

"Where did I go?" Jan's mother asked after she came into the room and turned around. We smiled at some of the funny things she said, even though we knew it was not funny at all. Jan's mother was in the beginning stages of Alzheimer's Disease.

"You are *not my daughter!*" she would tell Jan.

As Jan's mother went through each new stage, Jan's heart broke in a new spot. "I watched her make the last stitches as she finished a quilt for my little granddaughter," Jan recalls. "I hovered over her as she hugged the stuffed bear a neighbor brought her. I cried as she looked at me with blank eyes and saw a tear roll down her cheek."

Day after day, then year after year, we struggled with all the "why" questions.

"Mom didn't have an easy childhood," Jan recalls. "When her father wanted something at the table, he grunted. He never used words with the children, he just expected them to jump and figure out what he wanted. And her stepmother demanded that she do all the chores, take care of the younger children, and never, ever wear out her shoes."

And now this.

"So many times in those last few years, as I left Mom's bedside where she lay curled up in a fetal position, all I could think was, *It's not supposed to end this way!* I prayed over her and prayed over her, but the bedsores just got worse. We tried different nursing homes, but they were all awful. And we watched helplessly as my dad wore down with the burden of it all."

Jan had always expected that her parents would spend their final hours lying in their own bed, peacefully listening as all the kids said their last goodbyes. "Nothing could have been further from what was going on," she said. "And I couldn't do a thing."

Jan remembers her dad's oft-repeated words: "There's always something you can do about it." It's a wonderful attitude. An "I can" attitude is a great motivator that encourages us to take responsibility for what can be done. But there is a fallacy in that philosophy. The fact is, there are many things in life about which nothing, *absolutely nothing,* can be done.

Imagine a beautiful butterfly dipping down and landing on your hand. You could grab it and hold it tight, but what good would that be? How much better to open your hand and let it soar off. When we say goodbye to our disappointments, we are opening our hands and letting the disappointments go. We are letting God do His will in our lives.

Notes

Chapter 1
1. Rosalie Maggio, compiler, *The Beacon Book of Quotations by Women* (Boston, Mass.: Beacon Press, 1992), 348.
2. Phillip Yancey, *Disappointment with God* (Grand Rapids, Mich.: Zondervan, 1988), 2.
3. Colette Dowling, *The Cinderella Complex* (New York: Pocket Books, 1982).

Chapter 2
1. Judith Viorst, "The Thing I Regret Most Is _____ ," *Redbook,* June 1986, 60.
2. Barbra Minar, *Unrealistic Expectations* (Wheaton, Ill.: Victor Books, 1990), 51.
3. Betty Friedan, *The Feminine Mystique* (New York: Norton, 1983).

Chapter 3
1. Minar, *Unrealistic Expectations,* 52.
2. Lee Ezell, *The Cinderella Syndrome* (Eugene, Ore.: Harvest House, 1985), 57.

Chapter 4
1. James P. Comer, M.D., "Hopes and Dreams," *Parents Magazine,* Dec. 1990, 193.
2. Edmond Rostand, *La Princesse Lointaine,* Act 1, Scene 4.

Chapter 5
1. Judith Viorst, *Necessary Losses* (New York: Simon and Schuster, 1986).
2. Cheri Fuller, *Motivating Your Kids from Crayons to Career* (Tulsa: Honor Books, 1990), 60, 62.
3. Available through the National Association for Mental Health, Inc., Rosslyn, Virginia.

4. Sherry Suib Cohen, "The American Dream," *Ladies' Home Journal*, July 1986, 105, 132.

Chapter 6
1. William Bridges, *Transitions* (Reading, Mass.: Addison-Wesley, 1980).

Chapter 8
1. Dowling, *The Cinderella Complex*.
2. James Dobson, *Emotions—Can You Trust Them?* (Ventura, Calif.: Regal Books, 1980), 88–89.
3. David Stoop and Steve Arterburn, *Angry Man* (Dallas, TX: Word, 1991).
4. Dobson, *Emotions*, 86.
5. Neil Clark Warren, *Make Anger Your Ally* (Garden City, New York: Doubleday, 1983), 97–98.
6. *Random House Dictionary* (New York: Random House, 1991).
7. Minar, *Unrealistic Expectations*, 50–51.
8. Ellen McGrath, Gwendolyn Puryear Keita, Bonnie R. Strickland, Nancy Felipe Russo, Editors, *Women and Depression* (Washington, D.C.: American Psychological Association, 1990), xxii.
9. McGrath, *Women and Depression*, 48.
10. McGrath, *Women and Depression*, xii.
11. Maggio, *The Beacon Book of Quotations by Women*, 79.
12. Florence Littauer, *Dare to Dream* (Waco, Tex.: Word, 1991), 317.
13. Warren, *Make Anger Your Ally*, 21.
14. Harriet Lerner, *The Dance of Anger* (New York: Harper & Row, 1985), 71.

Chapter 9
1. Chuck Swindoll, *Growing Strong in the Seasons of Life* (Portland, Ore.: Multnomah Press, 1983), 350–351.

Chapter 10
1. Lewis Smedes, *Forgive and Forget: Healing the Hurts We Don't Deserve* (San Francisco: Harper Collins, 1991), 141.